CM0032066I

British Ferries

David L. Williams

Ian Allan
PUBLISHING

Front cover:
The French-built Sealink (British Rail) ferry *Horsa* at Folkestone, July 1976. Later renamed *Stena Horsa*, she was finally sold in 1992 when the Folkestone–Boulogne service was wound up. *John Edgington*

Back cover:
Reine Astrid, of Belgian Marine Administration, at Dover in September 1969. *John Edgington*

Title page:
The *Viking Valiant*, lead-ship of the 'Super Viking' class, sailing from Portsmouth, with Gosport in the background. The preserved former Royal Navy 'wooden-wall' *Foudroyant*, since relocated to Hartlepool, can be seen moored on the right-hand side. *David Reed*

CONTENTS

First published 2003

ISBN 0 7110 2891 5

All rights reserved. No part of this book may be reproduced or transmitted in any form or by any means, electronic or mechanical, including photocopying, recording or by any information storage and retrieval system, without permission from the Publisher in writing.

© Ian Allan Publishing Ltd 2003

Published by Ian Allan Publishing

an imprint of Ian Allan Publishing Ltd, Hersham, Surrey KT12 4RG. Printed by Ian Allan Printing Ltd, Hersham, Surrey KT12 4RG.

Code: 0306/B2

Acknowledgements

In appreciation of the assistance I have received in support of the preparation of this book, I should like to acknowledge the following organisations and individuals:

Chris Bancroft
Barry Carse
Alex Duncan
John Edgington
Leo van Ginderen
Laurence Liddle
Adrian K. Vicary (Maritime Photo Library)
David Reed
Dick Riley
Bettina Rohbrecht
Ian Shiffman
Don Smith
Ron Trowell
Henrik Vedel-Smith of the Statens Arkiver, Denmark
World Ship Society

Copies of certain colour pictures may be obtained from the following suppliers:
Bettina Rohbrecht at Diekwisch 10, D-22419 Hamburg, Germany, *and*
Don Smith at 7 Chapel Court, Hambleton, Selby, North Yorkshire, YO8 9YF.

Bibliography

Cowsill, Miles, and Hendy, John: *A Century of Ferries of North West Europe* (Ferry Publications, 1999)

Greenway, Ambrose: *A Century of Cross-Channel Passenger Ferries* (Ian Allan, 1981)
A Century of North Sea Passenger Steamers (Ian Allan, 1986)

Liddle, Laurence: *Passenger Ships of the Irish Sea, 1919-1969* (Colourpoint)

Pike, Dag: 'Ferries in Peril' (article in the *New Scientist*, 8 August 1985)

Robins, Nick: *Evolution of the British Ferry* (Ferry Publications, 1996)

Watson, Milton H.: *Disasters at Sea* (Patrick Stephens, 1995)

Winser, John de S.: *Short Sea: Long War* (World Ship Society, 1997)

plus numerous editions of Lloyds Register of Shipping and *Marine News* the journal of the World Ship Society)

INTRODUCTION

For all the changes that have arisen through its membership of the European Union, Great Britain remains an island nation. Despite the tenuous link with the Continent, in the form of the Channel Tunnel, the country remains detached from mainland Europe both physically and, to a large extent, spiritually. And, despite a growing network of international short-haul air services, we are still largely dependent on shipping transport for the bulk of the trading and travel links with our closest neighbours in Europe and Ireland.

At one time, barely 50 years ago, the cross-channel ferry services were the only means of getting to and from the Continent, across the Irish Sea and even to the various offshore islands of the Hebrides, Orkneys and Scillies, as well as to the Isle of Man and the Channel Islands.

The short-sea ferries themselves — the means by which this vital sea trade was maintained — were to some extent the 'Cinderellas' of the merchant navy. Inconspicuous and business-like, they lay between the grand and high-profile passenger liners of the inter-continental ocean routes, on the one hand, and the endearing 'butterfly' paddle steamers and small coastal ferries, on the other, tending to be overshadowed by both their larger and smaller cousins. Yet, in their day, the cross-channel steamers were as elegantly appointed as any Cunarder and were often described as 'mini-liners'.

Imagine public rooms styled on the baronial halls of country mansions, with open fireplaces and brocade-upholstered armchairs, Palm Court lounges, dining rooms with white linen tablecloths and silver cutlery, and cabins that were panelled in wood veneers and had double beds complete with counterpane covers. Such features, far removed from even the best of the accommodation of today's front-line ferries, were once the standard for premier class cross-channel passengers.

The fact was that, over 50 years ago, such grandeur remained fairly exclusive, the preserve of the well-off and of travelling businessmen, and this continued to be the case even for some years after World War 2. Thus it was that,

dictated by the traffic volumes as well as by the expectations of passengers of that era, a particular type of vessel had gradually evolved for the British short-sea routes, of modest tonnage but with accommodation of a quite luxurious standard.

Hull dimensions were governed by the need for a modicum of relief from *mal de mer*. Influenced by the sea behaviour of these waters and, in particular, the wave patterns that typically would be encountered throughout much of the year, hull lengths rarely exceeded 400ft. Engines — geared steam turbines or mighty diesels (adopted progressively from the late 1920s) — were reliable and powerful, to suit the unremitting demands of all-year-round schedules.

Today, of course, the ships of that specification are long gone, just like the era of which they were a part. Whatever we may think, the Britain of the 1950s is as remote to us today as the Edwardian era was to those who lived half a century ago. There is very little that now connects that time with the modern world, and it was the social and technological changes of the intervening years that swept away the traditional packet steamer, gradually replacing it with the kind of large, multi-role cross-channel ferry that is routinely operated today.

The principal change to the ships themselves has been in their expanding proportions — a phenomenon experienced with most other vessel types over recent times. Certain ferries operating today are significantly bigger in terms of gross tonnage than many of the ocean liners in service in the 1950s.

The other significant change to the characteristics of the short-sea ferry has been the transition from passenger-only vessels to dual-function passenger/vehicle ships with purpose-designed roll-on, roll-off loading facilities. Ferries of the latter type now operate exclusively on all routes.

So what were the forces that brought about such dramatic mutations in ferry design? In the 1950s the majority of the population, unable to afford anything more ambitious, still generally took their annual holidays in this country; for many,

this would be a week at the seaside at one of the many coastal resorts, all of which were still thriving. Most people had never been abroad, except, perhaps, with the armed services during wartime. For the few who could manage the extra cost to travel to the Continent for their vacation, this represented a measure of escape incomparable with any other experience, to the pleasures of foreign scenery and climate, to the intrigues of different national cultures as well as the mysteries of foreign languages and food, and alien currencies.

Within 10 or so years increased prosperity, brought about by improving pay levels and greater security of employment, provided the means for a growing sector of the population to indulge in these delights. Stimulated by growing aspirations to see the wider world, the demand for passage spaces soon made it necessary to introduce larger ships with increased cabin capacity. First manifest in the late 1950s, by the 1960s this had turned into a veritable travel explosion, launching a trend that was set to continue decade after decade and leading, ultimately, to cross-channel ferries of a size that were beyond anything remotely envisaged when services resumed after World War 2.

The dramatic effects of the upsurge in cross-channel travel can be readily demonstrated by a few simple statistics. There is little difference between the number of routes operated in 1950 and those maintained today, but the numbers of regular sailings on these routes have, on average, more than doubled. Indeed, on some of the English Channel and North Sea services, scheduled sailings have quadrupled; at the same time the passenger capacities of the ships themselves have in most cases increased at least twofold — all in all a growth of traffic volumes of more than 400%. By 1990 more than 20 million persons a year were making a short-sea crossing.

Simultaneous with the growth in passenger numbers, an unprecedented transport revolution was taking place as public transport (primarily the railways) was displaced by a more convenient form of private transport — the motor car. The introduction of a range of budget-priced models for the first time extended affordable car ownership to the masses. Not only did the car relieve the private passenger of dependence on domestic public transport systems for much routine travel; it also provided the means for horizons to be broadened,

offering the new-found freedom of independent leisure travel, which for many extended to excursions abroad. Thus, along with the extra passenger space required on the new generation of ferries, there was also a need for further adaptation in order to satisfy the demand for accompanied vehicle space, which was increasing in parallel.

Reflecting the changing composition of short-sea passenger traffic, as well as growing competition, fare structures were gradually modified too, being brought into line with what the new travelling public could afford. As a consequence, the high standards of accommodation and service previously enjoyed by a select passenger clientèle were no longer sustainable; in their place, tourist class cabins and amenities have gradually been adopted for the bulk of the passenger spaces, with only select areas set aside for those who still prefer to travel in premium accommodation.

Just as the nature of the cross-channel ships and the character of their passengers have changed beyond recognition over the past 50 years, so too the ownership and operation of these vessels has gone through something of a revolution.

Immediately after the war, shipping services were dominated by the railway operators and their state-owned associates — the 'Big Four' or British Railways in this country, and (among others) French National Railways (SNCF) and Belgian National Railways (SNCB) abroad. A number of Continental and British private operators also existed, but these were then in the minority. By the end of the 1960s, as 'Ro-Ro' services became firmly established, ownership was increasingly transferring from the public sector to private shipping companies. The squeeze on public expenditure during the high-inflation period of the 1970s was one of the key economic factors that had a bearing on this, accelerating the transition, as a prelude to complete de-nationalisation. Eventually, therefore, the independent operators came to dominate, with an emerging and significant presence by new Scandinavian concerns. As large, stylish, modern car ferries began to appear, heralding the super-ferries of just a short time later, amalgamations and partnerships also brought some big players onto the scene — notably P&O, whose passenger-shipping business had until then been confined largely to deep-water trading.

The last passenger-only ferry ordered by the United Steamship Co (DFDS) was the *Kronprinsesse Ingrid*. Later in life, from 1969, she had an equally successful career as the cruise ship *Mimika L*, looking as smart as she ever did. The *Kronprins Frederik*, her older consort, had a less auspicious experience after leaving DFDS: as the pilgrim carrier *Patra* she caught fire and sank in the Red Sea on 24 December 1976.
Don Smith

As the culmination of these unfolding developments to traffic patterns and service operation, the British Railways-owned short-sea fleet was finally sold into private ownership in 1984. Sealink (UK) Ltd, the operating company, was sold to James Sherwood's Sea Container Lines, functioning thereafter as Sealink British Ferries plc. Incredibly, as part of the disposal of this nationally-owned asset, 76 state-owned harbours, comprising 95 miles of quayside, were also sold off to private companies. It was the end of an era — the passing of the distinctive railway ferry services with their uniquely-styled ships, along with a series of classic boat trains — the 'Hook Continental', the 'Golden Arrow' and the 'Irish Mail', to name only the most famous.

The story of the 'Glory Days' of the British short-sea ferry is thus one of evolution, mapping the social changes of half a century. It tracks that period during which one form of vessel, quite small, yet magnificent and designed for a unique function appropriate to a particular era, gave way to another, very different but equally striking type of ship whose *raison d'être* is as much at variance with the role of its predecessors as the vessels are from each other.

Although this review does not extend to the present day, concentrating as it does on the period over which these various developments in British short-sea passenger shipping took place, the popularity of ferry crossing/self-drive holidays in Europe and Ireland is today as high as ever, experiencing year-on-year growth. It would seem, therefore, that the glory days of the British ferry are far from over!

1. BRITISH FERRIES — THE POSTWAR SCENE

The 1945 Labour Party manifesto promised the nationalisation of Britain's railways under a single authority, but, in the event, Clement Attlee's Government would be some three years into its term of office before it could implement this major industrial change. There were, of course, many who bemoaned such a radical policy swing away from private ownership of this key transportation sector, but in truth the Government was rescuing the four existing operating companies from virtual bankruptcy; in essence, the experiment of the 'Big Four' had not been entirely a success, for the scale of investment needed to maintain the infrastructure and rolling stock of each of these giant concerns was more than corporate balance sheets could endure.

Fifty years later, Britain's railway industry is once more privatised but is now in a parlous state. It could be argued that, in the intervening years, other than create a system to be proud of, we have simply gone full circle. There is, however, one exception to this — the short-sea ferry services operating around the British coast. Now maintained by various private shipping companies, they are thriving. Looking back with all the benefit of hindsight, perhaps it would have been better, all those years ago, if the postwar Labour Government, as part of its nationalisation programme, had done what modern business practice advocates and concentrated efforts on the core operation. Had it, right from the beginning, shed all the peripheral, non-track and train activities — shipping, road transport, catering services etc — and focused all investment on the essential railway operations, it might have been a

Among the very first ships to resume UK ferry operations after World War 2 was the LMS Railway's 1931-built, 2,838-gross-ton steamer *Princess Margaret*.
Ian Allan Library

different story today. As it was, for almost three years, those railway ferries which had survived the rigours of the recently ended war continued to operate under the flags of their respective 'Big Four' owners.

The short-sea ferry services on most routes had been suspended finally in early May 1940, although, as many cross-channel ships had been requisitioned for auxiliary military duties soon after the outbreak of World War 2, for all practical purposes most of the services had been wound down much earlier.

Restoration of commercial passenger services on the short-sea routes began in earnest even before the war had ended. The British & Irish Steam Packet Co vessel *Louth* was probably the first ferry to resume commercial schedules, commencing a temporary service between Heysham and Belfast on 14 December 1944, followed by the London, Midland & Scottish (LMS) Railway's *Princess Margaret*, which, having received only a limited refit, reinstated the Stranraer–Larne service on 25 December 1944. Both had been preceded by the Great Western Railway's *Great Western*, which recommenced commercial sailings in August 1944, but hers was a cargo-only service. The *Worthing*, a Southern Railway ship, opened up services on the South Coast, resuming sailings between Newhaven and Dieppe on 23 March 1945.

Following VE Day, the pace of resumption of passenger-carrying operations escalated rapidly. Another Southern Railway ship, the *Isle of Guernsey*, restored the Southampton–Channel Islands service on 25 June 1945. During that same month services were also restored between Liverpool and Douglas, Isle of Man, by vessels of the Isle of Man Steam Packet Co. Four months later, on 14 November 1945, the London & North Eastern Railway (LNER) ship *Prague* made the inaugural postwar sailing from Harwich to the Hook of Holland, thereafter maintaining a schedule of three round-trips each week. The *Duke of Lancaster*, one of three almost-identical ships built in 1928, rounded off a year of recovery when she restored the full LMS service from Heysham to Belfast on 13 December 1945. Earlier the same month, Burns & Laird Line's *Royal Scotsman* had done likewise on the Glasgow–Belfast route.

The rapid restoration of suspended short-sea passenger services continued throughout 1946 and into 1947, until by the end of that year virtually all the prewar short-sea passenger services had been reinstated, albeit with somewhat less tonnage than before, as the ships released by the Admiralty waited their turn for shipyard overhaul. While it would reveal the complexity of the network of ferry routes to and from the UK, a listing of all the reinstatements would be inappropriate here. Suffice to say that it took just over two years from the end of the war to get everything fully operational once more.

Despite the concerted efforts to reinstate the many cross-channel routes for peacetime passenger traffic, they remained fragmented for some time. Operators not only lacked adequate ships, as the survivors queued for shipyard attention, but were also hampered by gaps in their fleets caused by losses in the recent conflict. Some ships had been the victims of enemy action; others had been condemned to the scrapyard after hostilities had ended, being too run-down to justify the expense of refurbishment. As might be expected, some operators had fared better than others.

On the South Coast, the Southern Railway had lost eight of its ships, including the 1933-built *Brighton* from the Newhaven–Dieppe service and the *Maid of Kent*, sister to the *Isle of Thanet*, built for the Calais–Dover service in 1925. Twelve other Southern Railway vessels had, however, come through unscathed, helping the company to recover its services quickly. Of particular significance was the resumption, on 15 April 1946, of the Southern Railway's Dover–Calais crossing (and consequently its 'Golden Arrow' service to Paris), using the *Canterbury*. That October she was replaced on the run by the new *Invicta*, completed in 1940 but which was only now making her maiden commercial sailing. At 4,190 gross tons, the *Invicta* was the largest ferry on the Strait of Dover routes. Built by William Denny at Dumbarton, she was 384ft (117.1m) long and could carry 1,304 passengers in two classes in markedly superior accommodation.

For the Belgian Marine Administration the story was similar to that of the Southern Railway. Its most notable casualties had been the *Prince Leopold*, completed in 1929, and the new *Prince Philippe*, which sank following a collision on 15 July 1941, without ever entering commercial service

The *Canterbury*, owned by British Railways Southern Region, seen at Dover in April 1965. Nineteen years earlier she had reopened the Southern Railway's 'Golden Arrow' Dover–Calais service.
John Edgington

Constructed for Southern Railway's prestigious 'Golden Arrow' London–Paris through service, the *Invicta* finally fulfilled her intended role in October 1946, after a six-year delay caused by the war. She is seen at Dover in May 1966, painted in the new British Rail corporate colours.
John Edgington

across the Strait of Dover. The latter ship's two 3,300-gross-ton sister motorships, *Prince Baudouin* (1934) and *Prins Albert* (1937), were, however, soon restored to their postwar schedules. In the event, it was the *Prince Baudouin* that reopened the Ostend–Dover route on 24 July 1946 — a commemorative crossing which celebrated the centenary of that particular service.

Both Belgian Marine and the Southern Railway took prompt measures to replace their lost tonnage. For the Ostend–Dover route two new diesel-engined ferries, similar to Belgian Marine's prewar trio, were ordered from Cockerill Ougrée, Hoboken. Launched on 11 June 1946, the first of the pair, the 3,701-gross-ton *Koning Albert*, entered service in January 1948. Her sister, named *Prince Philippe*, joined her

six months later. In overall length they measured 372ft (113.4m) — the same as the prewar class of motorships.

On its Southampton routes, to fill the gap left by the *Normannia* (1912), sunk in May 1940, the Southern Railway contracted William Denny, Dumbarton, to build the single-funnelled *Falaise*. At 3,710 gross tons and measuring 311ft (94.8m), she made her maiden sailing from Southampton to St Malo in June 1947. More replacement ships were soon in the pipeline, among them the *Brighton*, the *Maid of Orleans* and a new *Normannia*, all named to commemorate wartime casualties.

The war had been disastrous for the other principal South Coast operators — the French national carrier SNCF (Société Nationale des Chemins de Fer Français) and SAGA (Société

▼ Completed in 1937, the *Prins Albert* was one of three motorships — the first to be owned by Belgian Marine — placed on the Ostend–Dover route prior to World War 2. Here she sails from Folkestone in July 1967. *John Edgington*

▲ The *Isle of Thanet*, which entered the Dover–Calais service in July 1925, also occasionally served the Folkestone–Boulogne route. Her sister, the *Maid of Kent*, was sunk by German aircraft at Dieppe on 21 May 1940. *Ian Allan Library*

◄ Presenting a nostalgic image of cross-Channel ferry operations over 50 years ago, the *Canterbury* arrives at Dover on 10 April 1946 after completion of her postwar refit. *Southern Railway*

Belgian Marine's *Prince Baudouin* was the fastest motorship in the world when completed in 1934. Built at the yard of John Cockerill, at Seraing, Belgium, she was retired in 1964 and purchased for use as an accommodation ship on the Ghent–Terneuzen Canal. *Ian Allan Library*

When completed in 1940 the *Invicta* was the largest ferry so far built for the Strait of Dover crossing. Her wartime career, commenced after two years spent laid up, was in the role of Infantry Landing Ship. The dark paint of her lower hull was later taken up to main-deck level, extending forward to her bow from just beneath the bridge, as shown in the picture on page 8. *Skyfotos*

At full speed on 26 July 1947, Southern Railway's new ferry *Falaise* shows her original appearance. *Ian Allan Library*

Cross-channel ferries had been active, making excursions, long before the recently-ended war. The poster advertises a programme of cruises in 1958 by BR Southern Region's 10-year-old *Falaise*. Rouen apart, most of her cruise destinations were the same as those of her scheduled-service sailings. *Bert Moody collection*

WEEK-END

Cruises

TO HAVRE

ROUEN

FROM £10·10·0 INCLUSIVE

ST. MALO AND

THE CHANNEL ISLANDS

SOUTHERN

S.S. FALAISE 1958 PROGRAMME

Anonyme de Gerance et d'Armament). The latter company's two Calais–Dover ships *Côte d'Argent* and *Côte d'Azur*, built in 1930 and 1932, had been badly damaged in 1940 while assisting in the evacuation of France and abandoned in French ports. Subsequently pressed into service by the German Navy as the *Ostmark* and *Elsass* respectively, both were sunk later in the war, preventing an early resumption of services across the Strait following the declaration of peace. Equally, SNCF was unable to re-deploy other vessels formerly owned by its predecessors, because their age and condition precluded the significant expenditure that would have been necessary to restore them to anything like an acceptable standard for commercial operation. The company did, however, have the 2,404-gross-ton *Londres* (ex-*Dieppe*), another wartime-completed ship which had survived Axis auxiliary employment from 1943 after she emerged from the Forges et Chantiers de la Méditerranée shipyard. She finally launched her commercial career on the Dieppe–Newhaven run on 11 April 1947, being joined that same season by her 2,600-gross-ton sister *Arromanches* (started as the *Newhaven*), whose interrupted construction was recommenced after the war. Geared turbine vessels capable of a speed of 24 knots, the pair measured 309ft (94.2m) registered length.

▲ Berthed at Newhaven on 15 June 1963, the *Londres* entered service on the Channel routes on 18 April 1946, after wartime service for the Germans as the minelayer *Lothringen*.
John Edgington

◀ The *Arromanches*, sister of the *Londres*, at Newhaven. She too provided wartime service to the German forces, under the name *Vichy*.
John Edgington

Typical of a number of prewar ferries that survived the war, the *Prague* — photographed here on 24 November 1945 — was one of three vessels introduced on the Harwich–Hook of Holland night service from 1929 by the LNER. Although fire brought her revived career to an early end, her owners continued to operate her sister *Vienna* in a joint operation with the General Steam Navigation-managed *Empire Parkeston*, ferrying troops across the North Sea under contract to the Ministry of Transport.
Ian Allan Library

The SNCF steamer *Arromanches* dressed overall, alongside the quayside at Dover on 7 March 1950, on the occasion of the state visit to Great Britain by the President of France, Monsieur Vincent Auriol.
British Railways

The postwar circumstances of the ferry companies working the North Sea reflected equally mixed wartime vicissitudes. Worst-off by the end of the war was probably the LNER, which retained just two ships fit for return to service, out of its prewar fleet of 11 vessels. Six of its ships had been sunk by enemy action; three others were either retained by the Government or judged to be beyond economic recovery. Barely three years after the cessation of hostilities, on 17 March 1948, one of the two survivors, the *Prague*, was destroyed in a major shipyard fire. Declared a constructive total loss, she was broken up.

As a first step in plugging the gap left by its heavy losses, the LNER immediately ordered the large new ferry *Arnhem*, measuring 4,891 gross tons and 377ft (114.9m) in length, from John Brown. She entered service in the summer of 1947, maintaining an unbalanced schedule on the Harwich–Hook of Holland route until the similar but larger *Amsterdam*, also built on Clydebank by John Brown, joined her in May 1951. In the interim, thanks to the creation of British Railways, the British Transport Commission transferred the

Outward-bound in the iced-over River Orwell in January 1963, during the very severe winter of that year, the *Koningin Emma* makes the day service sailing to the Hook of Holland from Harwich's Parkeston quay. The *Koningin Emma* and her Zeeland Steamship Co sister, *Prinses Beatrix*, looked noticeably different after their postwar refits, compared with their appearance on delivery from the de Schelde shipyard, Flushing, back in 1939.
G. R. Mortimer

Duke of York (1935) from the Irish Sea to the Harwich station, permitting the continuation of a service closer to the scale of the prewar operations. Rebuilt in 1950 with a single funnel, the *Duke of York* was at the same time converted to oil firing.

Across the North Sea, the Zeeland Steamship Co (Zeeland Stoomvaart Maatschappij) had recommenced the daytime Hook of Holland–Harwich service on 24 October 1946 with the *Oranje Nassau*, joined the following year by the *Mecklenburg*. The company had lost the 20-year-old *Prinses Juliana* off Flushing on 12 May 1940, but its new diesel consorts *Koningin Emma* and *Prinses Beatrix*, both completed in 1939 by K. M. de Schelde, were back in operation on the Flushing–Harwich route by the spring of 1948 after completing relief work in the Dutch East Indies — one of the remotest wartime deployments of any of the short-sea passenger ships. These modern-styled motor vessels (the first in the Zeeland fleet), capable of 22 knots, had a gross tonnage of 4,353 and a length overall of 380ft (115.9m).

Of the various Scandinavian ferry shipping concerns, some had also suffered from German seizure of their vessels, latterly

Bergen Line's *Venus* as reconstructed after World War 2. She was equipped with stabilisers for the longer, often rough crossing of the North Sea from Bergen to Newcastle, which she later maintained in the summer months alone.
Ian Allan Library

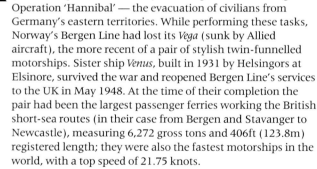

(in the early months of 1945) for transport duties during Operation 'Hannibal' — the evacuation of civilians from Germany's eastern territories. While performing these tasks, Norway's Bergen Line had lost its *Vega* (sunk by Allied aircraft), the more recent of a pair of stylish twin-funnelled motorships. Sister ship *Venus*, built in 1931 by Helsingors at Elsinore, survived the war and reopened Bergen Line's services to the UK in May 1948. At the time of their completion the pair had been the largest passenger ferries working the British short-sea routes (in their case from Bergen and Stavanger to Newcastle), measuring 6,272 gross tons and 406ft (123.8m) registered length; they were also the fastest motorships in the world, with a top speed of 21.75 knots.

The fleet of the other principal Norwegian ferry concern, Fred Olsen Line, had been left seriously depleted, four of its front-line passenger vessels having fallen victim to the fighting, including its newest constructions, the 5,035-gross-ton sisters *Black Prince* and *Black Watch*, which had been commissioned only in 1938. Olsen's Oslo–Grangemouth/Newcastle service was reopened in 1945 with the *Bali* (ex-*Alnwick*), built 1923, and the former Antwerp-route ship

Bretagne, a 1937-built motorship of 3,285 gross tons and 314ft (95.7m) length.

Although kept idle during the years of conflict, the ships of Swedish Lloyd (Svenska Lloyd), registered under the neutral flag of Sweden, had, equally, been spared exposure to military action. The company's *Britannia* and *Suecia*, sister steamships built by Swan Hunter & Wigham Richardson at Wallsend-on-Tyne in 1929, had resumed the Gothenburg–Harwich/London service in 1946. Measuring 4,216 gross tons and 376ft (114.6m) overall length, they had introduced superior accommodation on the Scandinavia–UK routes (prompting Bergen Line, in response, to commission the *Venus* and *Vega*). The *Britannia* and *Suecia* were joined, during that inaugural postwar season, by the company's new *Saga*, a somewhat larger motorship. Begun in 1940 by Lindholmens A/B but left incomplete for the duration, she was completed by Gotaverken A/B, Gothenburg, and made her maiden voyage on 20 May 1946, becoming the largest vessel up to that date to berth in London's Upper Pool. The *Saga* had a gross tonnage of 6,458 and an overall length of 421ft (128.4m) and could carry 340 cabin passengers in three classes.

The United Steamship Co (Det Forenede Dampskibs-Selskab A/S, or DFDS for short), the Danish ferry operator on the North Sea routes, had suffered wartime disruptions comparable to those experienced by the Norwegian concerns. Three of its four 'Parkeston'-class ships, introduced between 1925 and 1932, had been sunk, the *Esbjerg* after the cessation of hostilities, on 25 July 1945, when she struck a mine while *en route* to Copenhagen for her postwar refit. The sole survivor of the group, the *Parkeston*, re-entered the Esbjerg–Harwich service on 4 December 1945. She was notable as the first diesel-engined cross-channel ferry on any UK route when completed in 1925.

DFDS's *Kronprins Frederik*, another ship whose construction had been interrupted by the outbreak of war, was completed in short order by the Helsingors shipyard, Elsinore. She entered service in June 1946, extending the Denmark–UK route from Copenhagen as far as London. The *Kronprins Frederik* was another motorship, as was her later sister, *Kronprinsesse Ingrid*, completed in June 1949. Distinctive vessels, they looked every bit like scaled-down liners; tonnage was 3,895 gross, and overall length 375ft (114.3m).

Swedish Lloyd's *Suecia* is towed through one of the entrance locks of the Royal Docks group, London, by the William Watkins tug *Kenia*, in a photograph taken on 23 September 1957.
R. C. Riley

The DFDS *Parkeston* of 1925, the very first ferry on the UK routes to be powered by internal combustion engines. She measured 2,763 gross tons and 324ft (98.8m) length overall.
Statens Arkiver, Denmark

Built by Cammell Laird in 1932 for the Fishguard–Rosslare service, the reconditioned *St. Andrew* prepares to resume her peacetime ferry duties in 1947. Some years later, the white letters 'FR' (of the Fishguard & Rosslare Railways & Harbour Co) were added to the sides of her funnel.
Ian Allan Library

Still under Great Western Railway ownership, the *St. Julien* leaves Weymouth shortly after World War 2 with a full load of passengers bound for the Channel Islands. She maintained the service with her sister *St. Helier*.
Great Western Railway

Restoration of ferry services across the Irish Sea was beset by similar problems to those that afflicted operators in other regions. Here, as on the North Sea, there was a mix of railway- and privately-owned ferry fleets, each of which had to overcome vessel shortages brought about by the recently-ended war.

The London, Midland & Scottish Railway had been fortunate in not losing any of its original 'Duke'-class ships, nor the later *Duke of York*, and, of the three 'Princesses' built for its Stranraer–Larne route, only the *Princess Victoria* had been sunk, during the Dunkirk evacuation. The Heysham–Belfast service was maintained by the three older 'Dukes' (*Duke of Argyll*, *Duke of Lancaster* and *Duke of Rothesay*),

◀ The lone survivor of the Belfast Steamship Co's trio of twin-funnelled motor ferries, the *Ulster Monarch* lies at Belfast in a view probably taken prewar. *Ian Allan Library*

building up to full strength by the autumn of 1947. To supplement the *Princess Margaret* and *Princess Maud*, a replacement ship was ordered as the new *Princess Victoria* — a stern-loading car ferry scheduled for delivery in 1947.

The Fishguard & Rosslare Railways & Harbours Co, which had enjoyed a long association with the Great Western Railway on the UK–Ireland run from Wales, had lost two of its passenger ferries in the war — the *St. Patrick* on 13 June 1941 and the *St. David* on 24 January 1944. Commercial sailings between Fishguard and Rosslare recommenced in May 1947, when the *St. Andrew*, dating from 1932 and the only survivor of the three-ship class, revived the service with the first postwar departure. Meanwhile, two replacement ships were ordered from Cammell Laird for delivery in 1947 and 1948. Steam-turbine vessels, capable of a service speed of 20 knots, they could carry 1,300 passengers. Christened to commemorate the wartime casualties, the new *St. David* measured 3,352 tons gross while the slightly larger *St. Patrick* had a gross tonnage of 3,482; both ships were 321ft (97.9m) in length.

With the Irish Sea services being run by the Fishguard & Rosslare Railways & Harbours Co, the Great Western Railway concentrated on the restoration of its Weymouth–Channel Islands service, which it achieved in the summer of 1946 with

the *St. Helier*. Less than three years later this route would come under the newly-formed British Railways' Southern Region, virtually ending the Western Region network's direct involvement with passenger shipping.

Working the Irish Sea routes from Liverpool, Glasgow and Ardrossan were the various ships of the independent Coast Lines Group, which had pioneered the adoption of diesel-engined ferries under the Red Ensign. Its was a story similar to that of the Royal Mail Group, which had introduced large motorships on the ocean-liner routes — such as the Royal Mail Line's *Asturias* and *Alcantara*, and the *Britannic* and *Georgic* of White Star. Extending the experiment to short-sea passenger ship construction, Harland & Wolff, Belfast produced a series of eight similar motorships for Coast Line subsidiaries.

The Belfast Steamship Co took delivery of three of the group — the only ones to be completed with two funnels — namely the *Ulster Monarch*, *Ulster Prince* and *Ulster Queen*. Burns & Laird Lines had the *Royal Scotsman* and *Royal Ulsterman*, while the *Innisfallen*, *Leinster* and *Munster* were registered with the British & Irish Steam Packet Co.

Four of the eight vessels did not survive the war. The Belfast Steamship Co, left only with the *Ulster Monarch*, was allocated the former *Leinster*, which, returned to service as the *Ulster Prince*,

The *Ulster Prince*, formerly the British & Irish Steam Packet's *Leinster*, in the colours of the Belfast Steamship Co. *Don Smith*

Completed in 1930, the *Lady of Mann* had a long career with the Isle of Man Steam Packet, finally retiring in the 1960s. For part of her life her hull was painted white. *Bettina Rohbrecht*

▲ made the first departure from Liverpool to Belfast on 28 February 1946. The *Leinster*'s sisters, *Munster* and *Innisfallen*, had both been lost, leaving the British & Irish Steam Packet Co without any passenger ferries by May 1945. The Burns & Laird pair, employed throughout in various auxiliary capacities, returned to their owners' Glasgow/Ardrossan–Belfast services in September 1946. A programme of new

construction saw most of the Coast Lines' war losses made good by the end of 1948.

Closing this review of the British short-sea ferry routes in the immediate postwar period, we take a brief look at the circumstances of the Isle of Man Steam Packet Co, which operated all-year-round ferry services on the holiday routes between Liverpool, Fleetwood, Ardrossan and Douglas using an extensive fleet of ferries. The war had deprived the company of five of its fleet of 11 passenger steamships, four being sunk and one not returned to commercial service. Among the losses were the almost-new sisters *Tynwald* and *Fenella*, introduced in 1937. Ferry services to the island were reopened from the summer of 1945 using the *Lady of Mann* (1930) and *Ben-My-Chree* (1927), plus other older vessels. Within three years, however, thanks to an aggressive replacement programme, four new ships built by Cammell Laird — the *King Orry*, *Mona's Queen*, *Tynwald* and *Snaefell* — permitted the disposal of all but the most recent of the remaining prewar ferries. Of broadly similar size, these new ships measured around 2,490 gross tons and were 345ft (105.2m) long. By 1950 six vessels were sustaining daily sailing schedules to the Isle of Man with a combined capacity for some 9,000 passengers — a reflection of the traffic intensity on the Manx routes in those days!

With the short-sea routes more or less re-established and settled in by the end of 1947, the next big event to have a resounding impact upon the entire British passenger-ferry scene would be the formation of British Railways in January 1948.

2. THE CLASSIC YEARS — PART ONE: STATE-OWNED AND STATE-FUNDED SHIPS

Against much resistance (though little of it from within the industry), the Bill for the Nationalisation of the Railways received the assent of King George VI on 6 August 1947 and came into effect as an Act of Parliament on 1 January 1948. From the point of view of the paying customer, the formation of British Railways did not constitute as drastic a change to the system as might, perhaps, have been anticipated at the time. The four private companies were essentially re-designated as the Regions of the new national network, with the addition of a Scottish Region, comprising the track, station and shipping interests of the former LNER and LMS north of the border. Thus, Great Western became the Western Region, Southern Railway the Southern Region and so on. The Regions were controlled by six Railway Executives — the English operations of the LNER having been split into two Regions — later reduced to five when the Eastern and North Eastern Regions were again combined.

Aside from moves to synchronise and standardise across the entire network, with common fare structures and global timetables, the other principal advantage of the amalgamation was the freedom to move rolling stock from one Region to another, to smooth out shortages or to provide additional capacity where it was most needed, particularly during the difficult years of postwar recovery. As it was for the locomotives and railway carriages, so it was too for the railway-owned ferries. On the face of it, the changes that occurred were not huge, but changes there were.

The Great Western's Weymouth–Channel Islands service fell, geographically, within the boundaries of the new Southern Region, which accordingly took over the operation, along with two of the former Great Western steamers — the *St. Helier* and the *St. Julien*. The *St. Patrick* — a new vessel ordered after the war by Great Western — entered service in the very month that the nationalised network came into being, registered with

◀ The new *St. Patrick*, the third cross-channel steamer to bear this name, completed by Cammell Laird in 1947, and viewed from across a misty Newhaven Harbour in September 1971.
John Edgington

≪ 21

The Channel Islands ferry *St. Patrick*. Sold in 1971, she became the *Thermopylae*, later transferring to Agapitos Brothers as the *Agapitos I*. Her sister, the *St. David*, was sold to Chandris in 1970. *Ian Allan Library*

the Fishguard & Rosslare Railways & Harbours Co (FRRH). At first she alternated between stations, operating on the Weymouth–Channel Islands run during the summer months and spending the winter as the reserve ship for the Holyhead–Dun Laoghaire route; this continued until December 1959, when she transferred permanently to the South Coast.

In fact, the British Transport Commission, the ultimate owner of the British Railways ships, held a stake in FRRH, as it did in Associated Humber Lines, which managed certain ships in the North East on its behalf. Those services which were integrated with carriers on the Continent, under arrangements which went back to long before the war, continued to function along the same lines as before. Thus SNCF-owned ships worked alongside their BR Southern Region counterparts across the Strait of Dover and on the Newhaven–Dieppe route, while the Zeeland Shipping Co operated the day service from the Hook of Holland to Harwich in conjunction with Eastern Region ships, which made the

corresponding night crossings. The ships of the Belgian Marine Administration continued to maintain the Ostend–Dover services, as it had done prior to the outbreak of hostilities.

The years immediately following the creation of British Railways saw a continuing programme of replacement and upgrading of the state-owned fleets, with some quite innovative vessels brought into service. This chapter and the next look at the pure passenger ferries introduced over the period from the late 1940s to the mid-1960s. For the ferries of this type, which were effectively the ultimate descendants of the original cross-channel packets, this was a terminal era. The last of their kind would be commissioned during these years, and some, overtaken by the unfolding developments, would survive on the UK routes for only a very few years.

Indeed, for the traditional passenger steamers, this was a period beset with difficulties right from the beginning. Well into the 1950s, it remained a time of austerity and national impoverishment. The war had exacted a heavy toll, both on the country's infrastructure and on the health of the national economy. With all railway shipping now in public ownership, requirements for new vessels had to compete with numerous other Government projects for funding from what was already an over-stretched public purse. Fortunately, thanks to their high standards of construction and the extensive refits that they had received, many prewar ships promised a good many more years of reliable service before they would need to be replaced. However, by the time the financial situation had improved, permitting the acceleration of rebuilding programmes, it had become evident that things were in a state of flux. The realisation that the demand for conveying private vehicles was already expanding during the 1950s led, increasingly, to the introduction of combined passenger/vehicle ships in preference to traditional ferries, and the passenger-only ferry fell into rapid decline. In the event, some 23 new state-owned passenger ferries were commissioned between 1948 and 1966, the majority (18) prior to 1958.

The routes across the English Channel and Strait of Dover, to France, benefited from five new passenger ferries — three British-built and two from French yards — all in service by the 1953 season. First out was the *Maid of Orleans*, another

▲ The British Railways Southern Region passenger mail ferry *Maid of Orleans* shows her paces in a picture taken on 11 July 1962.
British Railways

◀ The new SNCF ferry *Lisieux* arrives in Newhaven Harbour on 24 March 1953, at the end of her maiden crossing from Dieppe.
British Railways

After 17 years on the Newhaven–Dieppe route, the *Brighton* was sold in 1966 and renamed *La Duchesse de Bretagne*. She is seen here at Newhaven on 15 June 1963. *John Edgington*

SNCF's *Côte d'Azur*, of 1951, at Folkestone in April 1965. Ownership of French-flag cross-Channel ferries was a complicated affair, the majority of vessels being managed by British Railways under a sharing agreement that dated from 1863. Some moved between British and French registration. Modified in 1981, the revised agreement consolidated total ownership with SNCF. The *Côte d'Azur* herself was sold in 1973, being renamed first *Azure* and, later, *Marie F.* *John Edgington*

William Denny-built ship, which entered service on the Dover–Calais route on 23 June 1949. With a gross tonnage of 3,777 and an overall length of 341ft (104.0m), she could carry 1,404 passengers.

A year later, for its Newhaven–Dieppe service, the British Transport Commission introduced a replacement *Brighton*, yet another product of the William Denny yard at Dumbarton. The *Brighton* was on the small side, at just 2,875 gross tons and 311ft (94.8m) in length. She was a turbine steamship, as were the French-flag *Londres* and *Arromanches*, alongside which she worked, and the new *Lisieux*, which entered service early in 1953. Slightly larger, at 2,943 gross tons and 317ft (96.6m), the *Lisieux* was built by Forges et Chantiers de la Méditerranée, Le Havre. The *Lisieux* was one of the fastest Channel ships,

having achieved a maximum speed of 25.4 knots on her builder's trials and, with her distinctive Valensi-designed Strombus funnel (a vane-like, streamlined structure) looked very much like a scaled-down version of the new 3,998-gross-ton, 365ft (111.3m) *Côte d'Azur* from the same shipyard. Placed on the Calais–Dover route, the *Côte d'Azur* appeared in SAGA colours when she entered service in August 1950, reverting to SNCF management less than a year later.

The last passenger-only ferry built for the cross-Channel link from Southampton was the *Normannia*, completed in January 1952 by William Denny as the replacement for the old *Hantonia*, which was then retired. With the previous *Normannia*, lost during the war, the *Hantonia* had pioneered steam-turbine propulsion for short-sea mail ships. The new

▲ Another British Railways Southern Region ship at Newhaven — the *Normannia* on 12 May 1968, after she had been converted into a stern-loading car carrier. *John Edgington*

The *Normannia* as built for the passenger-only Southampton–Le Havre crossing. Reconstruction as a car ferry involved an extension to her superstructure, forward of the bridge, its top serving as an additional open-air promenade area. Further aft, her lower saloon was sacrificed to provide the storage space for 111 vehicles. Her passenger capacity was simultaneously reduced from 1,400 to 500. *British Railways*

The 1948-built *Koning Albert*, one of two new diesel-engined mail ships introduced by Belgian Marine after World War 2. She continued in service until 1973, when she was laid up as reserve ship. The *Koning Albert* was broken up at Ghent from May 1978. Her sister, *Prince Philippe*, was renamed *Stromma Rex* for a short-lived Baltic operation, connecting Norrköping, Sweden, with Mariehamn, Finland. *Ian Allan Library*

vessel was a powerful-looking ship, distinguished from the similar *Falaise* by her flush-decked hull and higher super-structure — a look that arose from having a gross tonnage of 3,453 on a relatively short hull, just 309ft (94.8m) long overall. The *Normannia* was placed on the Le Havre service, occasionally relieving Eastern Region vessels on the Harwich–Hook route, and was one of the representatives of the British Railways fleet at the Coronation Naval Review in June 1953. Her passenger role was short-lived, however; just 11 years later she was converted into a stern-loading car ferry by Hawthorn Leslie at Hebburn-on-Tyne. The *Falaise* was similarly modified in 1964, the work being carried out by Vickers Armstrong at its Palmer Hebburn yard. Both vessels were employed thereafter as car ferries on the Dover–Calais run.

Belgian Marine Administration's introduction of the new motorships *Prince Philippe* and *Koning Albert* had been timely, for it was to suffer an unfortunate loss of one of its older ships, the *Prinses Astrid*, on 22 June 1949. When some three miles off Dunkirk, *en route* from Ostend to Dover, she ran on to an uncleared mine — one of the many laid during World War 2 which continued to be a menace to coastal shipping for some years afterwards. The explosion killed five of her 65-man crew, but there was no loss of life among the 218 passengers. Her master managed to run her onto a sandbank, but the 19-year-old ferry later broke in two and sank. On the face of it, the loss of the *Prinses Astrid* may not have been such a serious blow to her owner for, at the end of the following summer, one of her class-mates, the *Prinses Josephine Charlotte*, was also paid off for disposal, the name being transferred to a new car ferry that had been completed in 1949. Nevertheless, these departures — the one planned, the other unexpected — reduced the BMA passenger fleet to just five vessels. No steps were taken to remedy the deficiency, either — at least, not until halfway through the next decade.

The *Amsterdam*, near-sister to the *Arnhem*, was completed as a British Transport Commission ship, replacing the fire-destroyed *Prague*. The photograph shows her in the Clyde Estuary in June 1953. *British Railways*

The British Railways London Midland Region motorship *Hibernia* at Dun Laoghaire pier on 2 June 1949.
Ian Allan Library

Seen (*left*) immediately after her launch at Belfast, on 21 September 1948 is the second of the two new ferries for the Holyhead–Dun Laoghaire passenger mail service, the London Midland Region's *Cambria*, and (*below*) crossing the Irish Sea on 8 June 1961. At almost 5,000 gross tons, the *Cambria* and *Hibernia* were then among the largest short-sea ferries on the British register.
Ian Allan Library

The *Cambria*, still going strong in August 1970 — a photograph taken at Heysham. *John Edgington*

As the replacement for the gutted *Prague*, the John Brown-built 5,092-gross-ton *Amsterdam* — the new partner to the *Arnhem* — entered service on the overnight Harwich–Hook service in May 1950. Though virtually identical to her LNER-inspired sister ferry, the *Amsterdam* was ordered from the outset as a British Transport Commission ship. Both vessels were distinguished by a deep hull, with combined fo'c'sle and bridge deck extending almost to the stern, but the *Amsterdam* differed most noticeably from her consort in having her lifeboats carried aloft in gravity davits and had a deck house at the base of her foremast.

The first new BTC ships to be placed on the Irish Sea routes were the *Hibernia* and *Cambria*, resurrecting the names of two former London & North Western Railway ships. Among the largest new passenger ferries of their time, at 4,970 gross tons and 396ft (120.7m) in length, they entered the London Midland Region's Holyhead–Dun Laoghaire service in April

and May 1949 respectively, linking with the 'Irish Mail' express rail service from Euston. Squat and powerful-looking, the diesel-engined *Cambria* and *Hibernia* were both constructed by Harland & Wolff at Belfast. Accommodation on the pair was superior, befitting the contemporary standards aboard all new passenger ferries, in their case catering for 2,000 passengers. A peculiar feature, distinguishing them from BTC vessels on other sea routes, was a white line painted along the sides of their hulls, just below main-deck level.

The year 1953 witnessed a number of major accidents involving short-sea ferries, raising concerns about the safety of cross-channel vessels — a worry that has re-surfaced in more recent times. Among the victims of that season's unfortunate sequence of tragedies was the Eastern Region's *Duke of York*. On 6 May 1953 she was involved in a collision with the US-flag military cargo ship *Haiti Victory*, 40 miles from Harwich. There were eight deaths and numerous injuries

among those aboard the *Duke of York*, which lost her entire fore end in the impact. When rebuilt, the *Duke of York*, already modernised for the Harwich–Hook service, received a new flush-decked bow section with raked stem, increasing her overall length to 357ft (108.8m) and her gross tonnage to 4,325. She was back in service by February 1954.

Two years were to pass before two new classes of passenger ferry joined the state-owned shipping fleets, each comprising three ships — ambitious projects, given the wider turn of events. For the Belgium–UK routes, the Belgian Marine Administration commissioned a trio of striking motorships, their entry into service timed to coincide with an anticipated increase in traffic volumes associated with the Brussels World Fair of 1958. The trio were derived from earlier designs but were slightly larger. Like all Belgian Railways ships, they were nicely proportioned, similar to their predecessors but exhibiting modern features such as rounded bridge-fronts and streamlined Lascroux-type funnels, with smoke-clearance vents. With tonnage measurements of around 3,800 gross, they were 374ft (114.0m) long and were comfortably capable of a speed of 21 knots. First out, in July 1956, was the *Roi Leopold III*, followed by the *Koningin Elizabeth* in October 1957 and the *Reine Astrid* the following May. The last-named was the first ferry on the Eastern Channel routes to be fitted with stabilisers,

her consorts being similarly equipped at a later date. All three were built by Cockerill Ougrée. Stylish and appealing, they kept alive the concept of the traditional channel ferry …

… as did the three new turbine-powered passenger ferries introduced in 1956 by British Railways' London Midland Region for the Heysham–Belfast service. Replacing and adopting the names of three earlier 'Dukes', they were the *Duke of Lancaster* (August 1956), *Duke of Argyll* (September 1956) and *Duke of Rothesay* (January 1957), the first pair from Harland & Wolff and the last-named built by William Denny. Though virtually identical in length to the BMA trio, they were bigger ships, at around 4,800 gross tons, and looked quite different too. Compared with the low-lying, sleek appearance of the *Roi Leopold III* and her flush-decked sisters, the three 'Dukes' stood proudly out of the water. Powerful-looking ships with a three-island structure, they had a curved, raked stem and a single streamlined funnel fitted with a special smoke-dispersing appendage.

To replace the old *St. Helier* and *St. Julien*, still maintaining the Channel Islands service from Weymouth, the British Transport Commission contracted J. Samuel White, at Cowes, Isle of Wight, to construct the *Caesarea* and *Sarnia*. For their tonnage — 4,175 gross — these sisters had quite short hulls, of only 322ft (98.2m) length, and, as a consequence, exhibited

The *Reine Astrid*, sister to the *Roi Leopold III* and *Koningin Elizabeth*, leaving Dover on 22 June 1971.
British Railways

The Heysham–Belfast steamship *Duke of Argyll* alongside the Donegal Terminal, Belfast, in May 1970, after conversion into a passenger/car ferry. Her change of role has not drastically altered her external appearance. *British Railways*

Similarly modified, the *Duke of Rothesay* is seen after conversion into a car ferry in 1967, just 10 years after her entry into service. *British Railways*

Following conversion
into a car ferry, the *Duke of
Lancaster*, alongside at
Heysham in July 1965.
John Edgington

a rather dumpy appearance, various paint changes being tried
in a bid to enhance their looks. They were not dissimilar in
appearance to the *Normannia* and, like the earlier vessel, had
prominent raised bulwarks at the bow. In their case, though,
the plating was high at the stem and angled back sharply to
the foredeck.

Concurrent with the entry into service of the *Caesarea* and
Sarnia, on 2 December 1960 and 17 June 1961 respectively,
British Railways Southern Region closed its Southampton–
Channel Islands service, leaving the Weymouth link as the
only means of reaching the islands from the UK by sea. The
old *Isle of Guernsey* continued in service until 1969, but the *Isle
of Sark* was scrapped immediately following her withdrawal
in 1961; the *Isle of Jersey* had been sold for other employment
some years earlier.

Making her début the previous season was the last true
passenger ship destined for the Harwich–Hook route.
Commissioned by the Zeeland SS Co as the *Koningin Wilhelmina*,
in honour of the Dutch monarch who had abdicated in 1948,
she replaced the old *Mecklenburg*, which had given her owner
sterling service for just under 40 years. The *Koningin Wilhelmina*
was of a radical, modern design, her engines and funnel — a
squat, streamlined structure — being placed almost aft, giving
her a long, rakish fore section. She was by far the largest and

most spacious Dutch-registered ferry on the short-sea routes,
measuring 6,288 gross tons and 394ft (120.1m) in length
overall. Diesel-engined, with twin screws, she was built by
De Merwede at Hardinxveld. The *Koningin Wilhelmina*
commenced the North Sea day service on 7 February 1960
and would continue thus until 1979.

Apart from the *Mecklenburg*, *St. Helier* and *St. Julien* (the
latter pair actually surviving until 1966), a number of other
traditional passenger ferries disappeared from the short-sea
scene around this time. These included BMA's *Prince Charles* in
1960 and *Prince Baudouin* in 1964, along with the *Isle of Thanet*,
also in 1964, all destined for breaking. The *Britanny* found
continued employment from 1963 as the Viking Line's
Alandsfarjen, as did SNCF's *Londres* and *Arromanches*, which
were traded to Mediterranean owners in the same year and
renamed *Ionian II* and *Leto* respectively for their new roles.

The last conventional passenger ferry to be ordered by the
British Transport Commission (itself soon to pass away) — or,
for that matter, any UK-flag operator — was the *Avalon*, which
entered service for British Railways' Eastern Region on
25 July 1963 as the replacement for the ageing *Duke of York*.
Ironically, she had been launched by the wife of Dr Richard
Beeching, the Chairman of British Railways, only months
before he became instrumental in commencing the run-down

The *Caesarea* in April 1965, after she had received the new British Rail corporate colour scheme. *British Railways*

The *Sarnia* on builders' trials on 8 June 1961. After closure of British Rail's Channel Islands services, she filled in on various routes until 1978 when she became the *Aquamart*. Later the same year, she was acquired by the Greek owner Strombakis, converted for stern loading of vehicles and renamed *Golden Star*. *Ron Trowell — J. Samuel White Archives*

The design of the *Koningin Wilhelmina* was a dramatic departure from the exterior style of cross-channel ferries up to that time. Classed as a passenger ship, she could stow some 30-40 cars via side doors. The *Koningin Wilhelmina* spent 19 years on the Harwich–Hook service, until sold to new owners in 1979. She was first renamed *Captain Constantinos*, becoming the *Panagia Tinoy* two years later. *Don Smith*

The *Sarnia* at Weymouth in July 1964. *John Edgington*

The *Prinses Paola* of Belgian Marine — the last passenger-only ferry to be placed on the UK's ferry routes. In 1987, at the end of a long career on the Ostend–Dover route (and by which time she was the only surviving vessel of her type), she was traded for further service as the *Tropicana*. *Don Smith*

The cruise-ferry *Avalon* wearing the new 'Sealink' name and logo. She was converted into a car ferry after just 11 seasons as a pure passenger vessel. *Don Smith*

1975 at the end of a £1 million adaptation into a stern-loading car ferry. She was placed on the Irish Sea station, replacing the *Caledonian Princess* on the Fishguard–Rosslare run; she later worked between Holyhead and Dun Laoghaire, continuing with these duties until 1979, but her stern-loading configuration made her increasingly unsuitable in the face of mounting traffic volumes. At the end of 1980 she sailed to shipbreakers at Gadani Beach, near Karachi, ending a relatively short career.

The last pure passenger ferry to enter service with a state-owned operator — indeed the last of her kind for any operator on the UK routes — was the Belgian Marine Administration's *Prinses Paola*, completed in 1966. Given the wholesale migration to accompanied vehicle passages, her introduction constituted an expression of faith in the continuation of the passenger-only cross-Channel option and, as it turned out, an astute piece of commercial judgement, for she remained running successfully in this service, quite unaltered, until 1987.

Like other short-sea ferries under the Belgian flag, the *Prinses Paola* was very stylish. Constructed by Cockerill Ougrée, she had a gross tonnage of 4,356 and a length of 385ft (117.4m), making her the largest passenger-only vessel ever to be placed on the Dover routes. Despite her greater size, passenger capacity (at 1,700) was more or less the same as that of her earlier fleet-mates; however, reflecting her flagship status, cabin accommodation was superior, with 600 berthed in first-rate facilities, among them eight cabins graded as either 'de luxe' or 'special'. Propulsion was by turbocharged diesels driving twin screws, giving a comfortable service speed of 22 knots.

Despite the bold step of commissioning another pure passenger vessel during what was evidently the swansong era for this type of ship, thereafter no other ships for the ferry routes were built that did not have vehicle spaces and special loading features. Indeed, it was something of a surprise that the *Prinses Paola* survived on the Ostend–Dover route for as long as she did. Ultimately, though, she moved on, being transformed in the autumn of her career into the Mediterranean mini-cruise ship *Tropicana*. She served out her days carrying quite different passengers in far warmer climes, frequently encountering other former cross-channel ships in the course of her travels.

▲ of much of the railway network, precipitating its steepest period of postwar decline. Built at Linthouse, Glasgow, by Alexander Stephens & Sons, the *Avalon* had a gross tonnage of 6,584 and dimensions of 404ft (123.2m) overall length and 60ft (18.3m) beam. She could accommodate 750 passengers in total — 331 in First-class berths and 287 in Second-class berths; aircraft-type reclining seats were available for the remainder.

With an eye to the future, the *Avalon* was conceived as an off-peak cruise ship, operating an annual programme of cruises to Scandinavia and the Northern capitals and to Oporto, Lisbon and Gibraltar. With her dual role in mind, she was provided with high-grade public spaces and amenities, and, while engaged cruising, her accommodation converted into a single class for a maximum of 320 passengers. Nevertheless, like many ferries which were diverted to part-time cruising at that time (with the exception of those that were purpose-converted), the *Avalon* lacked the appointments and quality of state rooms that could be found for much the same outlay on true cruise ships. It was, perhaps, for this reason that the *Avalon* did not survive beyond 1974 in her original guise. At the end of that year she was taken in hand by Swan Hunter on Tyneside, re-emerging in the summer of gross tons and had an overall length of 374ft (114.0m). Diesel engines driving twin screws gave them a service speed of 17 knots — rather slow, compared with their Swedish and Norwegian contemporaries.

The *Braemar* went on to be the very last conventional North Sea passenger ferry to remain in service, lasting until 1975, when she was sold for more dubious employment as a casino ship, based in the Philippines. The *Blenheim* was less fortunate, having been seriously damaged in a fire on 21 May 1968 while some 200 miles east of Dundee. Her passengers were safely evacuated, but her condition did not warrant a full recovery for continued passenger-carrying duties, and she was converted into a car-carrier, surviving in this form until 1981.

Rival Norwegian concern the Bergen Line had reintroduced the twin-funnel *Venus* to the UK ferry service following a major refit which considerably changed her appearance. She too was engaged in cruises for part of the year, making excursions to Madeira and other Atlantic islands, as well as to the Mediterranean, the Norwegian Fjords and the North Cape. By the mid-1960s she had become a full-time cruise ship and, in keeping with her new role, adopted a modified colour scheme of white hull and upperworks and cream funnel with white bands.

Long before this, in 1953, when Bergen Line's main preoccupation was still the UK ferry service, the company brought out a vessel of comparable size as a belated replacement for the *Vega*, sunk in May 1945. There were no obvious visual similarities between the new ship, the 6,670-gross-ton turbine steamship *Leda*, and her twin-funnelled predecessors, but her design owed much to her heritage. Built by Swan Hunter & Wigham Richardson at Wallsend-on-Tyne, the *Leda* was an elegant vessel of distinctive appearance, characterised by a long fo'c'sle and a large, single raked funnel and tripod mast on top of her superstructure. Though she did not look especially modern, she featured the latest shipboard equipment and amenities and was the first North Sea passenger ship to be

fitted, as built, with stabilisers. Her accommodation for 403 passengers, predominantly in Tourist class, was of a high standard, and she too had hold space for up to 65 private cars. The *Leda* was bigger than both the *Venus* and *Vega* and also longer, with an overall length dimension of 437ft (133.2m). She entered the Bergen/Stavanger–Newcastle service in April 1953, making twice-weekly sailings all year round. In her second season she achieved a record crossing time for the route, making the Newcastle–Stavanger run in just over 16 hours. Following withdrawal in 1974 the *Leda* found new employment, first as a shipyard workers' accommodation ship and later converted as a dedicated cruise ship.

Danish operator DFDS did not introduce any more all-passenger ferries to complement its postwar-built motorships *Kronprins Frederik* and *Kronprinsesse Ingrid* on the Esbjerg–Harwich crossing. Indeed, it very nearly suffered a loss which would have reduced it to a single ship of this ranking, for the

▼ The *Kronprinsesse Ingrid*, seen here at Esbjerg, and her sister *Kronprins Frederik* truly looked like mini-liners. They were the last passenger-only ferries ordered by the United Steamship Co (DFDS). *Statens Arkiver, Denmark*

The *Innisfallen* of 1948, owned by the City of Cork Steam Packet, alongside her owner's dedicated berth at Cork. The *Leinster* and *Munster* of the British & Irish Steam Packet were very similar. All three ended up working in the Mediterranean for Greek owners — the *Innisfallen* as Latsis Lines' *Poseidonia*, and the *Leinster* and *Munster* with Epirotiki as the *Aphrodite* and *Orpheus* respectively. *Maritime Photo Library*

The distinctive glass-enclosed verandah, a unique feature of Fred Olsen's twin ships *Blenheim* and *Braemar*, can be clearly seen in this aft quarter view of the latter vessel. *World Ship Photo Library*

Kronprins Frederik was extensively damaged in an on-board fire while lying at her berth at Harwich on 19 April 1953. The inferno destroyed a third of her accommodation spaces and, worse still, the blazing vessel capsized away from the Parkeston quayside, as the result of the volumes of water pumped into her to extinguish the fire. Miraculously, after she had been raised and towed to Denmark, she was fully repaired and restored to service 12 months later; in the interim the older *Parkeston* was transferred from the Esbjerg–Newcastle service to fill in. In 1964 the *Parkeston* became a workers' accommodation ship, while the *Kronprins Frederik* was switched to the Faroes and Iceland route in 1966. After long careers with DFDS, both the *Kronprins Frederik* and the *Kronprinsesse Ingrid* saw further service with new owners, the former briefly as a Red Sea pilgrim ship (until sunk following another fire), the latter as a Mediterranean passenger ferry.

3. THE CLASSIC YEARS — PART TWO: INDEPENDENT OPERATORS

454ft (138.4m), making her the largest North Sea passenger ship so far built. Like her smaller running-mate, she was a magnificent vessel: all white, with the distinctive gold five-pointed star on a blue circle emblazoned on her funnel — a true mini-liner. She too worked the Harwich and London schedules, carrying just over 400 passengers in four classes. For First class the accommodation was superb, and the ship was generally very well appointed. At the other extreme, for the more thrifty, accommodation was provided in dormitories for the 64 passengers in the lowest fare grade.

The *Saga* and *Patricia* were, indeed, quite exceptional for short-sea ferries, but despite their evident qualities they were uneconomical to operate; Svenska Lloyd found it difficult to fill them when traffic volumes on the Scandinavian services fell sharply in the mid-1950s, and their duration on the short-sea schedules to the UK was thus rather short. Electing to retain the older, smaller-capacity *Suecia* and *Britannia*, which would survive for another nine years, Svenska Lloyd sold the newer ships

As it had been for passenger-only ferries of the state-owned shipping companies, so it was also, from the late 1940s to the mid-1960s, for those operated by the independent concerns. Progressively, they were replaced by car-carrying vessels — a process that accelerated as the years passed.

Concentrated on the North Sea routes from Scandinavia and on various routes across the Irish Sea, there were some 11 traditional packet vessels in service with private ferry companies at the beginning of this twilight period. Fleet-enhancement programmes saw another 20 new ships of the same type introduced over the 12 years from 1948.

The Scandinavian services were particularly competitive. With the popular steamships *Suecia* and *Britannia* once again maintaining the Gothenburg–London route, Svenska Lloyd introduced a bigger, turbine-powered consort for the 6,687-gross-ton motorship *Saga*, which had entered service in 1946. The new ship, the Swan Hunter-built *Patricia*, completed in 1951, measured 7,940 gross tons and had an overall length of

◄ Swedish-Lloyd's striking postwar *Saga* was engaged in the Gothenburg–London service from 1946. She was renamed *Ville de Bordeaux* by the French Line (CGT), which purchased her in 1957; eight years later she became the *Nessebar*.
Alex Duncan

▼ Equally pleasing in appearance was the *Saga*'s consort, the *Patricia* of 1951.
Alex Duncan

Fred Olsen's
modern-styled
Blenheim, introduced
on the Oslo-Newcastle
service in 1951 and
followed a year later by
sister *Braemar*.
Powerful, as well as
elegant in appearance,
their hulls were built
by Thornycroft at
Southampton with the
fitting-out undertaken at
Oslo after they had been
launched. They could
each carry 286
passengers. *Fred Olsen*

Issued by Norwegian
State Railways, this
Fred Olsen Line brochure
was published to promote
the entry into service of the
twin ferries *Blenheim* and
Braemar. *Bert Moody collection*

for other employment. Hamburg–Amerika Line took the *Patricia* in 1957 and converted her into the elegant 'pocket' cruise ship *Ariadne*; she enjoyed a cruising career that lasted into the 1980s, with several name changes after she left Hamburg–Amerika ownership in 1973. The *Saga* was also sold in 1957, to the Compagnie Générale Transatlantique (French Line), which placed her on a trans-Mediterranean service under the name *Ville de Bordeaux*.

Having sustained the Oslo–Grangemouth/Newcastle service with ships transferred from the Antwerp route, Fred Olsen Line finally introduced replacements for the war-lost *Black Prince* and *Black Watch* in 1951 and 1952. These took the form of the strikingly stylish and ultra-modern *Blenheim* and *Braemar*. Probably the most distinctive short-sea passenger vessels of their generation, they were beautifully proportioned, with sleek hull lines, a high curved and raked bow, streamlined aluminium superstructure (rounded at the bridge and the aft

end) and a contoured funnel with short extension at the leading edge. Particularly interesting was the glazed First-class verandah constructed at the aft end of the bridge-housing on the boat deck; curved horizontally and vertically into a quarter sphere, it overlooked the sea across clear deck space aft. In keeping with other ferries on the longer routes across the North Sea, the *Blenheim* and *Braemar* were fitted with stabilisers during the course of their careers. They were also air-conditioned throughout and featured saunas among their innovative passenger amenities.

These novel and elegant ships were partly British-built, the John I. Thornycroft yard at Southampton working in conjunction with Akers MV, Oslo, which installed their engines and fitted out their accommodation. First out was the *Blenheim*, which made her maiden sailing from Oslo and Kristiansand to Newcastle in February 1951, the *Braemar* joining her in May 1952. They could accommodate almost 300 passengers in three classes and could carry a small number of private cars, hoisted aboard and stowed in the holds. Besides their regular schedules, both ships were also employed on cruises during the off-peak months. They measured 4,776

Maintaining a significant presence on the postwar UK ferry scene were three ships sailing under the 'Hammer and Sickle' which operated a regular service between Leningrad and London, making calls *en route* at the Baltic ports of Helsinki, Gdynia and Copenhagen. The 7,494-gross-ton *Baltika*, formerly the *Vyacheslav Molotov*, inaugurated the service in 1946. She was joined by the *Mikhail Kalinin* from 1958 and, two years later, by a sister ship, the *Estonia* (seen here). All three were registered with the Baltic State Steamship Co, part of the huge Sovcomflot organisation — the state-owned fleet of Soviet merchant ships. The latter pair were modern motorships built at the Mathias Thesen Werft yard in Wismar, East Germany, the *Mikhail Kalinin* being the lead ship of the class which would ultimately comprise 19 ships employed on a variety of sea routes around the USSR. They had a tonnage of 4,870 gross and a length of 401ft (122.3m). *Alex Duncan*

Orders for new ships for the companies of the Coast Lines group were placed from 1946 onwards, essentially for a series of motor ferries which were more or less a continuation of the class of vessel first introduced from the late 1920s. All but one were constructed by Harland & Wolff at Belfast. They exhibited a family likeness to their forebears and generally were of comparable size and dimensions.

In 1948 the British & Irish Steam Packet took delivery of a pair of sister ships bearing the names *Leinster* and *Munster*. The old *Leinster* had been sunk in the war, while the former *Munster* had been transferred within the parent organisation, becoming the Belfast Steamship Co's *Ulster Prince*. The new ships were twin-screw motor vessels of around 4,000 gross tons with a hull length of 367ft (111.9m). Slightly smaller in size, at 3,705 gross tons, and 340ft (103.7m) in length, was a new *Innisfallen*, built by William Denny, which entered service the same year for the subsidiary City of Cork Steam Packet Co,

British & Irish Steam Packet's *Munster* of 1948, berthed at Liverpool. *Don Smith*

Bergen Line's last pure passenger ferry, the *Leda*, maintained the Bergen–Newcastle schedules for 21 years. After a period spent as an accommodation ship, she was sold in 1979, becoming the *Najila*. Later changes of ownership saw her renamed successively as the *Albatross*, *Allegro* and then *Albatross* for a second time, in 1985. *Ian Allan Library*

The Isle of Man Steam Packet ferry *Manxman*, sixth in a series of similar ships, made her debut on the Liverpool–Douglas route in 1955. *Bettina Rohbrecht*

Coast Lines' *Irish Coast*, built by Harland & Wolff, entered service in October 1952. Sold in 1968, she was transferred to the Mediterranean, where she continued in operation under a string of names until transferred to the Philippines, where she ran aground following a collision in October 1989. Partially cut up where she lay, she was later re-floated and demolition completed at Manila. *Don Smith*

Cruising was a popular form of employment pursued by both state and private ferry owners, and not always during off-peak times of year. The poster advertises cruises from Liverpool to the Scottish Lochs in 1953 by Coast Lines' 3,220-gross-ton *Lady Killarney*. Shore excursions included opportunities to play golf at ports of call. Inclusive fares ranged from 15 guineas for a six-day cruise in a four-berth cabin to 51 guineas for a 13-day cruise with single-room occupancy. *Bert Moody collection*

The *Scottish Coast*, the last conventional short-sea ferry to be commissioned by the Coast Lines group, painted in the colours of Burns & Laird Lines, which she served from the early 1960s. *Don Smith*

Following the *King Orry*, *Mona's Queen*, *Tynwald* and *Snaefell* — all of broadly similar tonnage and dimensions — the *Mona's Isle*, fifth in the series, entered service for the Isle of Man Steam Packet in 1951. *Alex Duncan*

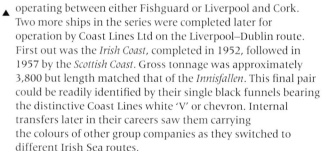

operating between either Fishguard or Liverpool and Cork. Two more ships in the series were completed later for operation by Coast Lines Ltd on the Liverpool–Dublin route. First out was the *Irish Coast*, completed in 1952, followed in 1957 by the *Scottish Coast*. Gross tonnage was approximately 3,800 but length matched that of the *Innisfallen*. This final pair could be readily identified by their single black funnels bearing the distinctive Coast Lines white 'V' or chevron. Internal transfers later in their careers saw them carrying the colours of other group companies as they switched to different Irish Sea routes.

The rapidly changing trading patterns on the short-sea ferry routes militated against long careers for the various passenger-only ships of the Coast Lines group. The prewar vessels were gradually disposed of for scrap, while by 1969 those introduced from 1948 onwards had all been sold for service in the Mediterranean, either for alternative, inter-island ferry duties or for conversion into mini-cruise ships.

Elsewhere on the UK's west coast, the Isle of Man Steam Packet was pursuing a similar line of fleet replacement and enhancement. Two more traditional ferries, of broadly the same category as the quartet commissioned between 1946 and 1948, were added to the company's fleet in the 1950s. The *Mona's Isle* entered service in 1951, followed by the *Manxman* four years later. Powered by steam turbines driving twin screws, their tonnage was 2,945 gross and their overall length 345ft (105.2m). In the early 1960s the Isle of Man Steam Packet finally made the transition to car ferries. From that time the older, pure passenger ships were progressively displaced as more car-carrying ships were commissioned. First to go were the old *Lady of Mann* and *Ben-My-Chree*, followed successively by the passenger ferries of the postwar era. By the beginning of the 1970s the Isle of Man service had become almost exclusively a Ro-Ro operation. There was no doubt about it — the future lay with vehicle ferries!

4. THE SHAPE OF THINGS TO COME

The Southern Railway had placed the first regular car-carrying ferry, the converted cargo ship *Autocarrier*, on the Strait of Dover route as early as 1931. This singular action could have been misconstrued as a demonstration of the Southern Railway's forward-looking vision and its commitment to providing for the private motorist, but this was far from the case. Like the other railway companies, its revenues were derived primarily from train passengers, and it had no desire to undermine this source of income by encouraging competition from alternative modes of transportation. The fact was that Captain Stuart Townsend (of the Townsend Bros shipping firm) had embarrassed the Southern Railway into launching its car service, for, when he found there were no existing ferry arrangements for conveying his private car to the Continent, he had established his own unscheduled operation using chartered vessels, challenging the Southern to respond.

In practice, of course, these early enterprises did not amount to much, apart from representing the birth of what eventually was to become a trade of phenomenal proportions and being the catalyst of a hostile competitive force that would ultimately be the undoing of railway shipping. The *Autocarrier* could convey only 35 cars. Likewise, the vessel

The Southern Railway's first special car-carrying passenger ferry, built in 1931 by D. & W. Henderson, Glasgow, was the *Autocarrier* (*left*) . The main picture shows the precarious method by which cars were loaded aboard her. (*both*) *Ian Allan Library*

engaged for Townsend's sporadic alternative service, the *Forde*, could accommodate just 28 private vehicles. Besides that, these tiny vessels were slow and offered little in the way of creature comforts in the cramped deck spaces for their human occupants. They were supplemented from 1936 by Belgian Marine's converted *London–Istanbul* (ex-*Ville de Liege*), the first side-loading car ferry. Prewar, these three ships amounted to the full extent of the provision for accompanied vehicles across the English Channel. But it was the hint, tiny as it was, of what the future held in prospect.

Perhaps the most significant prewar development in the new era of ferry transportation of private vehicles was the *Princess Victoria*, introduced by the London, Midland & Scottish Railway on the Stranraer–Larne route in July 1939. Apart from being the very first British ferry to be equipped as designed and built with a stern-loading car ramp, she was also the first UK-flag, railway-owned diesel-engined ship. Prior to this, and even for a long time afterwards, the conveyance of motor cars aboard ferry was a tortuous affair that brought furrows of consternation to the foreheads of owners and insurers alike. Cars had to be lifted aboard by crane — a risky business at the best of times, frequently

resulting in mishap. Furthermore, petrol tanks had to be completely drained prior to embarkation, leaving drivers with the worry of whether they would find a convenient source of replenishment fuel at their port of destination.

Immediately after World War 2, car-carrying ferry operations across the Strait of Dover resumed in earnest, although they remained relatively minor compared to the passenger business. Townsend placed the converted naval frigate *Halladale*, the first roll-on, roll-off (Ro-Ro) ferry, in service in 1950. The Southern Railway continued briefly with the old *Autocarrier* until the 1947 season, when she was replaced by the converted steamer *Dinard*, previously on the Southampton–Channel Islands–St Malo run, whereas Belgian Marine took the bold step of commissioning its first purpose-built car ferry, the *Car Ferry* (later renamed *Prinses Josephine Charlotte*), which entered service in 1949. A 2,537-gross-ton ship, measuring 373ft (113.7m) in length, the *Car Ferry*, unlike the *Dinard*, was capable of loading motor cars through her stern.

Returning to 1947, a replacement *Princess Victoria* had recommenced the Stranraer–Larne car ferry service for the LMS, her namesake having been a war loss on 19 May 1940, mined outside the entrance to the River Humber. The new *Princess Victoria* gave faultless service for five good years, maintaining a successful mixed operation, carrying, at maximum payload, 1,500 passengers and 40 private cars — only half the number of the previous ship. Constructed by William Denny, Dumbarton, the *Princess Victoria* was a modest-sized vessel at 2,694 gross tons and 323ft (98.5m) overall length — virtually a replica of the original ship of the name and very similar in overall appearance to the older, passenger-only ships *Princess Margaret* (1931) and *Princess Maud* (1934). Like her predecessor, though, she proved to be an unlucky ship.

For the short-sea routes to the UK, the unfolding 1953

Clearly revealing her naval origins, Townsend's 1,370-gross-ton, 302ft (92.1m) car ferry *Halladale*, formerly a 'River'-class frigate (K417) built by A. & J. Inglis in January 1944. Seen here in October 1950, she was sold in 1962 following the delivery of the *Free Enterprise*, becoming the *Norden* and, later, the *Turist Expressen*. *Maritime Photo Library*

After World War 2 the 2,291-gross-ton *Dinard*, built in 1924 for Southern Railway's overnight Southampton–Channel Islands service, was converted into a crane-loading passenger/car ferry with capacity for 80 cars. The photograph shows her on 14 July 1952. She was sold in 1958 for continued service in the Baltic, serving A/B Vikinglinjen under the name *Viking*, being the first ship to be owned by that company. Ironically the Viking Line would later establish a dominant presence on the Strait of Dover routes. *R. H. Tunstall*

Commissioned as the *Car Ferry*, Belgian Marine Administration's first purpose-built car-carrying ferry was renamed *Prinses Josephine Charlotte* in 1952. She is seen approaching Dover on 28 May 1971. *British Railways*

The two LMS passenger/car ferries named *Princess Victoria* were notable for quite different reasons.

The original, prewar vessel was the first specially-built stern-loading car ferry to be employed on any of the UK short-sea routes. Her near-identical successor, shown here, would suffer the first major disaster to a ferry with an unobstructed garage deck, in January 1953, when she was barely six years old.
Ian Allan Library

season proved to be both extraordinary and tragic, opening with a sequence of disasters involving cross-channel ferries — each with fatal consequences — two of which have already been described. Setting the tone for that unforgettable year, the first catastrophe witnessed the demise of the new *Princess Victoria*, in her case with terrible loss of life. While making a winter sailing from Stranraer to Larne on 31 January, the *Princess Victoria* was completely overwhelmed by an exceptional storm. Mayday signals were transmitted, but before aid could reach the scene, the stricken vessel had foundered. Aboard were 176 persons — 127 passengers and 49 crew — of whom a total of 134 lost their lives. Although it was not, perhaps, fully appreciated then, the *Princess Victoria* disaster was something of an early warning of the dangers to which cross-channel ferries were exposed — particularly those with un-partitioned decks, reached through doors in the hull. The subsequent investigations revealed that the calamity had occurred, in part, because of the failure of her stern doors, allowing her to flood and become unstable.

Back at Dover, the first car ferry to be completed to the specification of the British Transport Commission, designed and built from the outset for the carriage of motor-cars, was

introduced in 1952. This was the 3,333-gross-ton, 362ft (110.4m)-long *Lord Warden*. Also built at the Dumbarton yard of William Denny, she had capacity for 120 vehicles loaded through doors in her stern, and, like the *Princess Victoria* before her, represented something of a milestone in the development of the modern car ferry.

The following year, in June, a new drive-on Car Ferry Terminal, complete with Bailey-bridge-type linkspans, was opened in Dover's Eastern Docks. Equipped to handle simultaneously two stern-loading ferries, it set the standard for vehicle handling and was the culmination of a programme of engineering work at the Straits ports, similar developments having taken place at Calais and Ostend. Despite this (for the time being, at least), of the few car ferries by then in service, even fewer were stern-loaders. Loading cars through the ship's side or hoisting them into the holds by crane continued to be the 'norm' for most car ferries.

The 1950s were boom years, prompting Prime Minister Harold Macmillan to coin the election-winning phrase "You've never had it so good!" Austerity and rationing were fading memories, and there were more houses, refrigerators, vacuum cleaners and other household gadgets than ever before. Few people then had television to entertain themselves at home, and even fewer owned a car, but all that was changing rapidly, as, in parallel, were people's expectations.

The increasing pace of commercial demand resulting from these social advances was unprecedented, and one of its consequences was more car ferries, particularly across the Channel. Six years after the *Lord Warden* entered service she was joined by another new, streamlined car ferry, the motor-vessel *Artevelde* of Belgian Marine, working the Ostend run. Built by Cockerill Ougrée, the *Artevelde* measured 3,812 gross tons in size and 383ft (116.8m) in length overall, making her the largest car ferry based at Dover at the time of her inauguration. She could accommodate 160 cars along with 1,000 passengers.

Mention should also be made of the all-welded train ferry *Compiegne* that came out that same season (1958). The first vessel of this type owned by SNCF, she subsequently carried both motor and rail vehicles on the Calais–Dover route. Ordered from the Chargeurs Réunis Loire-Normandie shipyard, the 3,467-gross-ton *Compiegne* had an overall length of 377ft (114.9m).

Both the *Artevelde* and *Compiegne* had stern doors installed. Among the latter ship's novel features were bow thrusters, controllable-pitch propellers and a stern-mounted docking bridge. All in all, with their modern styling, the pair represented the general trend in vehicle-ferry design at that time.

Not to be outdone, the British Transport Commission introduced a consort to the *Lord Warden* in 1959. Another vessel which helped to advance the evolution of the British vehicle ferry was the 3,920-gross-ton *Maid of Kent*, as she was christened, she had a superior vehicle capacity over her fleet-mate, with space for 190 cars, and her shipboard passenger amenities were of the highest standard, in keeping with those found aboard contemporary traditional packet steamers. Yet

again the product of William Denny, she made her maiden sailing on the Dover–Boulogne route in May 1959.

The enquiry into the *Princess Victoria* disaster found no fault in the operation of the vessel but regrettably (given future occurrences) did not look critically at the emerging design of car-carrying vessels characterised by open vehicle decks which, if flooded, would seriously — even catastrophically — destabilise them. Attention was focussed instead on the ship's stern doors, which had proved to be worryingly insubstantial against the force of a full-blown storm.

Having awaited the outcome of the enquiry before deciding upon a replacement vessel, the British Transport Commission finally ordered a new ship for the Irish Sea crossing, this materialising in 1961 as the *Caledonian Princess*. Registered with the Caledonian Steam Packet Co — a wholly-owned subsidiary of the British Transport Commission — she was in many respects the model for subsequent British Railways car

▲ The British Railways Southern Region car ferry *Lord Warden*, undergoing sea trials on 15 May 1952. Like those of the *Princess Victoria*, her stern doors and access ramp (out of sight in this view) were of lightweight construction and did not even extend to main-deck level; they were subsequently strengthened to improve watertight integrity. *British Railways*

The *Maid of Kent* at Dover in May 1971 with *Normannia* alongside her and the multi-role (passenger/vehicle/train) ferry *Vortigern* next to the quay. The *Maid of Kent* joined British Railways' English Channel fleet in the 1959 season. *John Edgington*

Photographed at Weymouth in 1970, while working the Channel Islands schedules, the *Caledonian Princess* had previously maintained the Stranraer–Larne service. *John Edgington*

◄ Prior to the introduction of the *Free Enterprise*, Townsend Bros had either purchased second-hand tonnage or had operated vessels under charter. The rather innocuous-looking *Free Enterprise* was in fact a key vessel in the development of improved car-carrying operations on the UK ferry routes.
Don Smith

The SNCF car ferry *Compiegne*, a stylishly-designed vessel in keeping with many of the cross-Channel ships built during the 1950s for Continental operators. *Ian Allan Library*

Townsend's third purpose-built vessel, the 4,657-gross-ton *Free Enterprise III*, entered service in 1966 on the Dover–Zeebrugge route. The outline of her clam-shell bow door, running down the side of her hull from the fore deck, can be clearly seen. Her close sister *Free Enterprise II* later became the Isle of Man Steam Packet's *Mona's Isle*. *Ian Allan Library*

ferries introduced on routes around the UK over the next five or so years. This may have been something of a retrograde step, for, unlike the *Maid of Kent*, the *Caledonian Princess* could stow only 100 cars. Nevertheless, she was a larger vessel than the ship she was replacing, with a tonnage of 3,629 gross and a length of 353ft (107.6m) overall. A turbine-engined steamship, she was constructed by William Denny and made her maiden departure on the Stranraer–Larne route in November 1961.

In the meantime, Townsend Bros had been doggedly pursuing its private car-ferry revolution, targeting objectives that were dramatically ahead of contemporary thinking among the ranks of the nationalised operators. Hitherto, car-carrying ferries had strictly been foot-passenger ferries upon which some provision had been made for the conveyance of motor vehicles. The new approach, in contrast, was to concentrate primarily on the car-carrying dimension, with the passenger accommodation focussed on drivers and their travelling companions. In keeping with this, in April 1962, Townsend introduced on its Dover–Calais service the 2,607-gross-ton, 317ft (96.6m)-long *Free Enterprise*, so named to highlight the complete contrast in the philosophies then motivating ferry operation and development — the profit incentive of private capital vs the state funding of public ownership. She was the lead ship of a radically advanced series, all from the NV Gusto Werft shipyard at Schiedam, which, in retrospect, have come to be regarded as the vessels that launched the next generation of car ferries. Although she too was a stern-loader, she had much higher car capacity and greater 'tween-decks headroom, in anticipation of commercial vehicle traffic.

Around this time, British Railways was contemplating withdrawing completely from its base at Southampton, ending all cross-Channel ferry services from there to Le Havre and Cherbourg. Rumour became reality in May 1964, bringing to an end 120 years of continuous service on these routes. However, waiting in the wings, ready to fill the vacuum, was Norwegian ship-owner Otto Thoresen. Thoresen considered that, with the right ships and frequency of service, the Southampton routes still had great potential, particularly as he proposed to exploit both passenger and vehicular traffic.

◀ Berthed at Southampton, the *Viking I* has her bow and stern doors open, permitting a clear view through the entire length of her vehicle deck. It was this drive-through capability — not provided by contemporary railway ships — that so revolutionised cross-channel car-ferry operations.
Ian Allan Library

Thus it was that Thoresen Car Ferries pioneered the introduction of drive-through dual-role car ferries on the United Kingdom's sea routes, beginning with the 3,608-gross-ton *Viking I*, which entered service in May 1964. This was in all respects a revolutionary vessel, with up-and-over clam-shell bow door in addition to a stern vehicle door. Cars were accommodated on two decks, which incorporated dedicated areas with adequate headroom for trucks. Her engine-room exhausts were split and taken up the ship's side to vent at the edges of her decks, allowing more room for vehicles to manoeuvre and permitting the design of more appealing open passenger spaces. Quite apart from offering more competitive fares than those previously charged by British Railways, Thoresen also guaranteed a seat for every passenger.

TOWNSEND THORESEN

VIKING I

Seen here in the colours of
the combined Townsend-
Thoresen company,
the *Viking I* was the first
drive-through car ferry to
operate a service from a
British port. *Don Smith*

Where British Railways had been making steady losses,
the Thoresen enterprise generated a respectable profit,
right from its very first season. A second, almost identical
ship, the *Viking II*, was added to the service in July 1964,
built, like her sister, at the Kaldnes M/V A/S shipyard at
Tönsberg; the third of the class, the *Viking III*, which followed
in June 1965, was built by Orenstein-Koppel at Lübeck,
West Germany. Measuring 3,821 gross tons, she was diesel-
engined, like the first two *Vikings*. Each had an overall
length of 326ft (99.4m) and could carry 180 cars along with
approximately 1,000 passengers. The 'Vikings' had an
enormous impact, in a sense launching another
Scandinavian invasion of Great Britain.

Simultaneous with these events, Townsend — very much a
kindred spirit of Thoresen — had brought out the first of its
own bow and stern-loading ferries, the 4,122-gross-ton, 355ft
(108.2m)-long *Free Enterprise II* — the first true, built-from-
scratch, drive-through car ferry on the British register —
which made her début in May 1965. She was swiftly followed
by six more, similar ships, the later vessels being somewhat
larger, at around 5,000 gross tons, and longer, at 386ft
(117.7m) overall.

At a stroke, these new Townsend and Thoresen ships had
rendered obsolete the railway-operated car ferries — even
the very latest, extremely stylish Belgian Marine vessel, the
Koningin Fabiola, which entered service in the 1963 season.
Spurred into action by the recognition that many more
vessels would be required to satisfy the evidently booming
demand for motoring holidays abroad, British Rail began to
convert a number of its passenger-only ships into car ferries,
but it was now a question of responding to a whole new
league of competition.

◄ The train ferry *Saint Germain*, built in 1951 for the 'Night Ferry' through rail service from London Victoria, via Dover and Dunkirk, to the Gare du Nord, Paris, is seen at Dover in April 1965. By then she was carrying road vehicles as well as railway carriages, her clear decks readily lending themselves to adaptation for this purpose. The later train ferries *Vortigern* and *St. Eloi* were similarly adapted to convey vehicular traffic. *John Edgington*

▼ Following the *Artevelde* of 1958, Belgian Marine's next passenger/car ferry was the *Koningin Fabiola*, introduced in 1963. Here she is painted in the Sealink colour scheme of Regie voor Transports Maritiem. *Don Smith*

FERRY INTERIORS

Just like the ships themselves, the interiors of the short-sea ferries have undergone a dramatic transformation over the period covered by this book. These pictures feature accommodation aboard typical vessels completed in each of the decades following the end of World War 2, revealing styles ranging from manorial splendour to space-age simplicity.

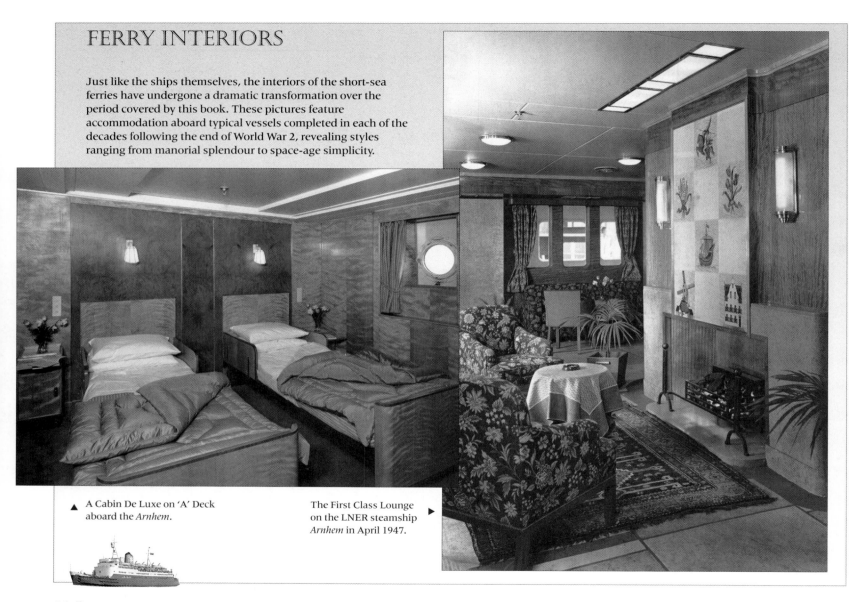

▲ A Cabin De Luxe on 'A' Deck aboard the *Arnhem*.

The First Class Lounge on the LNER steamship *Arnhem* in April 1947. ▶

The First Class Smoking Room on the Southern Railway's *Falaise* in July 1947.

A Cabin De Luxe in First Class on the *Normannia* in February 1952.

The A La Carte Restaurant of the *Brighton*, completed in 1950 for British Railways' Southern Region.

The Smokeroom aboard the *Caledonian Princess* of 1962.

▲ The First Class Bar aboard the *St. Columba* in 1977.

▲ The Second Class Bar of the *St. Edmund* in 1974.

all pictures in this feature from the Ian Allan Library

5. THE TIMES THEY ARE A'CHANGING

As Bob Dylan's song stated, when it entered the charts, appropriately enough, in March 1965, 'The Times They Are A'Changing'. For the UK's ferry trade, they most certainly were!

As already noted, prompted by the realisation that the pattern of UK ferry travel was shifting unalterably away from foot passengers alone towards accompanied vehicle traffic, the various state-owned shipping operators instigated measures to remedy the deficiencies in their respective fleets. New ships would, of course, take some time to bring into service; furthermore, those already on order were committed to designs that remained far from ideal in the circumstances and that would inevitably result in further restrictions in capacity. Having to balance the conflict of interests between their railway and ferry operations presented the railway operators with a fundamental dilemma, but at least they were now, as ferry operators, attempting to fulfil their obligations to meet customers' expectations.

Short-term action by the British Railways Board involved the conversion of a number of its older, all-passenger vessels into car-carriers, including some of the ships displaced by the recent closure of the cross-Channel routes from Southampton. The *St. David* was taken in hand for adaptation in 1963, followed by the *Normannia* and *Falaise* a year later. From the Irish Sea routes, the *Duke of Argyll* and the *Duke of Lancaster* were likewise converted, in their case into stern-loaders, but the *Duke of Rothesay* became a side-loader when she was modified later.

The British Railways Board was not the only railway shipping concern that had been left standing by the rapid turn of events. Belgian Marine was committed to the construction of a class of new car ferries, beginning with the 3,745-gross-ton, 385ft (117.4m)-long *Koningin Fabiola* in 1963, but these vessels were oudated in design concept. Elegant and visually striking though they were, they were nevertheless hybrids envisaged with 1950s traffic levels in mind. Similarly, the new 3,400-gross-ton *Valençay*, *Villandry* and *Chantilly*, completed for SNCF in 1964/5, had to be modified later.

The problem was not confined to state-owned operators; certain of the private shipping concerns had also been caught napping. Coast Lines would have no ships suitable for ferrying cars until after 1966, and the Isle of Man Steam Packet, having finally elected to commence a vehicular ferry service with its *Manx Maid* of 1963, had fallen into the same trap by commissioning a vessel that was virtually obsolete before she even commenced sailings on the Liverpool–Douglas route. To help position cars in readiness for disembarkation, a revolving turntable had been installed on her car deck whereby vehicles were rotated to face the stern doors; while this was something of an improvement, loading remained a slow process. Even so, three similar ships were to follow.

Although Townsend's and Thoresen's drive-through ships were the trend-setters of the first wave of modern car ferries, other new ship designs still constituted something of a mixed bag, and the introduction of vessels featuring superseded vehicle-handling facilities continued for a good many more years — well into the 1970s. Among these were a small number completed as side-loaders, such as the beautifully-proportioned, 8,221-gross-ton *England*, built for DFDS by Helsingör S&M in 1964. Taking advantage of the three-year interval between their construction, her sister-ship, the 8,658-gross-ton *Winston Churchill*, was modified prior to completion and entered service, in May 1967, as a stern-loading ship. While both ships were of 460ft (140.2m) length overall, their respective vehicle capacities were 100 (increased to 120 in 1974) and 180. A comparison of the time taken to load and unload each ship would have made a more revealing illustration of the benefits of the pre-service enhancement to the later of this pair.

The majority of the passenger car ferries introduced between 1965 and 1975 were either of the drive-through variety (with bow and stern ramps) or stern-loading, the numbers of each being roughly equal. However, the stern doors installed aboard all these vessels, of both types, were of a completely new configuration, influenced by the findings

The DFDS-owned *England*, one of the most attractive ferries to work on the British routes. Unfortunately, her elegant external design concealed a far-from-ideal car-handling layout. Loading was through side doors placed well aft *(left)* which had limited-headroom access, restricting vehicle accommodation to private cars, towed caravans and touring vehicles.
B. Coaley/Ian Allan Library

The converted passenger/car ferry *Duke of Lancaster* at Belfast in May 1970. *John Edgington*

The first ferry to be completed for the Isle of Man Steam Packet to have car-carrying capabilities was the stern-loading *Manx Maid*, delivered in 1963. She had a tonnage of 2,724 gross and an overall length of 344ft (104.9m). *Don Smith*

DFDS

MV ENGLAND
MV WINSTON CHURCHILL

Awaiting your pleasure.... To convey you in comfort and ease between Harwich (Parkeston Quay) and Esbjerg. Relax and enjoy the bracing atmosphere of a passage by sea in a superb ship.

Tickets and further information:

▲ The elegant *Winston Churchill*, owned by United Steamship Co (DFDS), Denmark, operated on the Esbjerg–Harwich route until 1983, for the final five years serving as a relief boat. *Don Smith*

◄ The front cover of a DFDS brochure featuring its two new ships for the Harwich–Esbjerg car-ferry service, with the *England*, the first of the pair, as its centrepiece. *Bert Moody collection*

Strike-bound in Newhaven on 10 June 1966, the converted passenger/car ferry *Falaise*.
Brian Stephenson

The *Dover*, viewed at Newhaven in September 1970. *John Edgington*

The *Holyhead Ferry I* manœuvres alongside the quay at Dun Laoghaire in July 1970, ready to unload vehicles over her stern ramp. *John Edgington*

of the enquiry into the *Princess Victoria* disaster. Unlike the relatively lightweight, horizontally-closing twin gates of the *Princess Victoria*, the stern doors on these new ships were rugged structures, operating as a single unit (hinged or one-piece) through a vertical arc and locking into position to form an integral part of the watertight hull. It is important to stress that in none of the later flooding incidents involving vehicle ferries was failure of the stern doors a contributory factor.

Given that the split between roll-through and stern-loading car ferries in this era was approximately 50:50, it perhaps comes as no surprise to learn that virtually all the former type were commissioned by private operators, whereas the stern-loaders were predominantly delivered to the state-controlled and railway concerns.

Of similar general design to the *Caledonian Princess*, the *Dover* and the *Holyhead Ferry I* entered service for British Railways in 1965, the first on the Strait of Dover crossing, the other on the Holyhead–Dun Laoghaire route. Both ships were built at

The *Earl Leofric* — the former *Holyhead Ferry I* — at Calais on 5 September 1980 following conversion into a drive-through ferry, with her new clam-shell bow door shown in the raised position. *Richard Capper*

Belgian Marine's *Roi Baudouin*, photographed on 10 May 1968. Engaged on the Ostend–Harwich car-ferry service, she is about to make her first docking at the British Rail portal berth at Parkeston Quay. *Ian Allan Library*

Newcastle, by Swan Hunter and Hawthorn Leslie respectively. They entered service as stern-loading vessels but were subsequently converted — an expensive business — to roll-through layout, at the same time receiving, respectively, the new names *Earl Siward* and *Earl Leofric*.

To the *Koningin Fabiola*, Belgian Marine added the similar *Roi Baudouin* in 1965 and *Princesse Astrid* in 1968. Though marginally improved as car carriers, the later pair could accommodate only 160 cars and provided just 95m of deck space for road-haulage vehicles, in contrast to the 180 cars and 165m allowed for trucks aboard the smaller and shorter Thoresen 'Viking' class and Townsend 'Free Enterprise' ships; their passenger numbers were also lower. Five larger Belgian Marine ships built in the 1970s had vehicle capacities that were somewhat better but still much lower than the opposition's.

Simultaneous with the *Dover* and the *Holyhead Ferry I*, SNCF had brought out the similar but smaller *Valençay* and *Villandry* for the Dieppe–Newhaven service, followed by the slightly larger and improved *Chantilly* for the Calais–Dover crossing. As already noted, these ships would also require subsequent modification to increase capacity and facilitate faster turnarounds, yet follow-on classes of railway ferries for the cross-Channel routes continued to retain inherent design weaknesses when compared with their private counterparts.

Perhaps unsurprisingly, in this climate, the 1960s witnessed

◀ Outward-bound in Southampton Water in 1982, the Townsend-Thoresen *Free Enterprise V* passes Calshot Spit. *David L. Williams*

▼ SNCF's new car ferry *Chantilly* entered service in 1966. Completed as a stern-loading car ferry, she was converted to drive-through configuration during the winter of 1976/7. *Ian Allan Library*

The SNCF's *Valençay* arriving at Newhaven in July 1965. Along with sister *Villandry* she was modified by the addition of a clam-shell bow door and bow ramp at the same time as the *Chantilly*. *British Railways*

Painted in DFDS Prins Ferries colours, the 5,829-gross-ton *Prinz Hamlet* and her sister *Prinz Oberon*, maintained the 20-hour Harwich–Bremerhaven/Hamburg crossing which the first *Prins Hamlet* had opened in May 1966. The photograph dates from 27 October 1981 — shortly after the absorption of Prins Lines by DFDS. Each of these ferries had capacity for 1,100 passengers and 210 private cars. *Ian Allan Library*

The 9,500-gross-ton, 465ft (141.8m)-long *Jupiter*, photographed at Newcastle on 2 July 1966, at the end of her maiden voyage from Bergen. She and her sister *Venus* were the first car ferries to serve Norway. They were also among the most interesting of UK ferries, spending the summer months of each year, under these names, running Bergen Line's North Sea ferry service; for the rest of the year they operated cruises under the Fred Olsen banner — hence the *Jupiter*'s colour scheme — bearing the alternative names *Black Watch* and *Black Prince* respectively. *Ian Allan Library*

the first wave of encroachment on the UK's short-sea routes of new, mainly foreign-flag, private shipping concerns ready to exploit the evident shortcomings of the existing ferry operators. In the wake of Thoresen, the German concern Prins Ferries launched a Hamburg–Harwich service in the summer of 1966, inaugurated with the large, modern drive-through car ferry *Prins Hamlet*. This 8,688-gross-ton, 441ft (134.3m) vessel — sold shortly after as the *Roussillon* — was followed by the smaller, stern-loading *Prins Oberon* in June 1970 and a second *Prinz Hamlet* in 1973, the *Prins Oberon* becoming the *Prinz Oberon* in 1978. Switched subsequently to a Bremerhaven route, they later came under the DFDS banner when Prins Ferries was absorbed in 1981.

In the mid-1960s various jointly-owned multi-national ferry concerns were formed, commencing new operations across the North Sea, the Irish Sea and the English Channel. Of particular interest, the structure of each company included an element of P&O

among its partner concerns, bringing this major player onto the short-sea ferry shipping stage for the first time.

North Sea Ferries was established in 1966 as a consortium of P&O subsidiary General Steam Navigation and British, German and Dutch partners, including the Dutch Royal Nedlloyd concern. Its first ships were the roll-through ferries *Norwave* and *Norwind* — inelegant ships of 4,300 gross tons and 359ft (109.5m) length, built at Bremerhaven by AG

The Wilson Line (Ellerman's Wilson Line, to give it its full name) brought out its final UK ferry, the Cammell Laird-built *Spero* in August 1966. With a tonnage of 6,916 gross and measuring 454ft (138.4m) in length overall, she replaced the *Borodino*, the company's last passenger-only ferry, introduced in 1950, on the Hull–Copenhagen route. *Ian Allan Library*

Passing The Needles rocks off the eastern tip of the Isle of Wight, inward-bound for Southampton, the *Dragon* lacks any operator's name painted on her side. The view dates from around the late 1960s, when she was owned by General Steam Navigation, a P&O subsidiary. *Ian Allan Library*

'Weser' Seebeckwerk. Maintaining a service linking Hull with Rotterdam's Europoort, they rivalled the state-owned ships on other North Sea routes and later plugged the gap on the Zeebrugge service left by the withdrawal of Wilson Line's *Spero*. Zeeland Shipping Co reacted with its stylish *Koningin Juliana*, brought out in 1968, while the British Railways Board responded with new ships of its own for the Harwich–Hook night service.

On the South Coast, General Steam Navigation again represented P&O as a principal collaborator in another partnership with SAGA and Irish associates, creating Normandy Ferries, which commenced services linking Le Havre with Southampton and Rosslare in 1967. The operation was maintained by the sister ferries *Dragon* (UK flag) and *Leopard* (French flag). Measuring approximately 6,100 gross tons and 442ft (134.6m) in overall length, both were constructed in French shipyards. Their début constituted the first rivalry between private operators — certainly on the South Coast, where Thoresen was already working these routes with its 'Viking' ships.

Competition for ferry passages from Southampton intensified in 1971, when Swedish Lloyd based its attractive sister ships *Hispania* (ex-*Svea*), *Patricia* and *Saga* at the Hampshire port, sailing to Bilbao in Spain. Transferred from the Gothenburg–Tilbury route, for which they had been constructed, the Swedish trio were considerably larger than their Thoresen and Normandy Ferries counterparts, at over 8,500 gross tons and 463ft (141.2m) in length — measurements reflected in their greater car capacity of some 300 each. Surprisingly, passengers — all berthed, of course — were limited in number to 408. Nevertheless, with the arrival of these ships, ferry traffic from Southampton had reached almost saturation point, and something had to give. In the event, the Swedish ships, which fared the least well, were soon withdrawn; unable to fill their car decks, they were incapable of handling the plentiful lorry traffic that was becoming available. Their departure from the Southampton scene signified the decline in Swedish Lloyd's involvement in the UK ferry services.

Elsewhere, P&O also became involved in the Irish Sea services, presaging its complete takeover of the Coast Lines group of ferry companies in 1971.

Throughout the decade from the mid-'60s to the mid-'70s the trend-setters remained Townsend and Thoresen, the two companies eventually merging in 1968 to form the most formidable international ferry/shipping concern on the UK routes. Hot on the heels of the last 'Free Enterprise'-class ship — the *Free Enterprise VIII*, which appeared in 1974 — the newly-formed Townsend-Thoresen Ferries prepared to launch a renewed assault on the ferry trade in the form

North Sea Ferries'
Hull–Rotterdam service
was opened in 1965 with
the sisters *Norwind*, shown
here, and *Norwave*. They were
roll-on, roll-off double-deck
car ferries, the first of their
kind on North Sea crossings.
Alex Duncan

of its 'Super Viking' series of ships, among the first of the next generation of vehicle ferries. As an indication of the superior design qualities of both of the 'Free Enterprise' and 'Super Viking' classes, the majority have continued in service until recent times as members of the later P&O European Ferries fleet.

For other concerns, it remained a case of catch-up. Coast Lines, soon to be swallowed up by P&O, had finally placed its first car ferries in service on the Irish Sea routes — the new *Ulster Prince* and *Ulster Queen*, on behalf of the Belfast Steamship Co, and the distinctively-styled drive-through vessels *Innisfallen*, *Munster* and *Leinster*, which entered service in 1968 and 1969 for B+I Line (the reincarnation of the British & Irish Steam Packet). The *Munster* and *Innisfallen* were built by Werft Nobiskrug at Rendsburg, but the *Leinster* was the product of the Verolme shipyard at Cork. The trio, virtually identical, had a tonnage of 4,850 gross and an overall length of 388ft (118.3m).

Although the majority of the ferries constructed in this period were motor vessels, the transition from steam was not complete until the Isle of Man Steam Packet finally abandoned steamships in the early 1970s — the last ferry company to do so. Having taken delivery of the turbine-powered *Ben-My-Chree*, sister to the *Manx Maid*, in 1967, it was compelled, finally, to bow to operating pressures in order to keep its fuel costs down, and the follow-on duo — the *Mona's Queen* of 1972 and the *Lady of Mann* of 1976 — were fitted with diesel engines.

At the very point when the UK ferry scene was set to hot-up yet again, with the emergence of the second generation of vehicle-carrying vessels, another new contender appeared on the scene in 1973. Britanny Ferries — an independent French company with modest beginnings — depended initially on second-hand tonnage for its ferry schedules from Caen and St Malo to Portsmouth, but it was to feature prominently on the short-sea stage in the not-too-distant future.

Swedish Lloyd's beautiful *Patricia*, completed in March 1967 by Lindholmens Varvet A/B, Gothenburg. Her duration on the UK short-sea routes, along with that of sisters *Saga* and *Hispania* (ex-*Svea*), was relatively short. Placed initially on the Tilbury–Gothenburg route, they were later transferred to a Southampton–Bilbao service. *Bettina Rohbrecht*

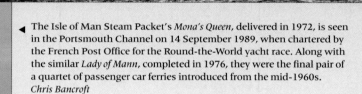

The Isle of Man Steam Packet's *Mona's Queen*, delivered in 1972, is seen in the Portsmouth Channel on 14 September 1989, when chartered by the French Post Office for the Round-the-World yacht race. Along with the similar *Lady of Mann*, completed in 1976, they were the final pair of a quartet of passenger car ferries introduced from the mid-1960s. *Chris Bancroft*

The distinctive styling of the Coast Lines group's *Innisfallen* of 1969 — a look shared with her sister B+I Line car ferries *Leinster* and *Munster* — can be seen here to good effect. The funnel shape was described as a 'witch's hat'. *Bettina Rohbrecht*

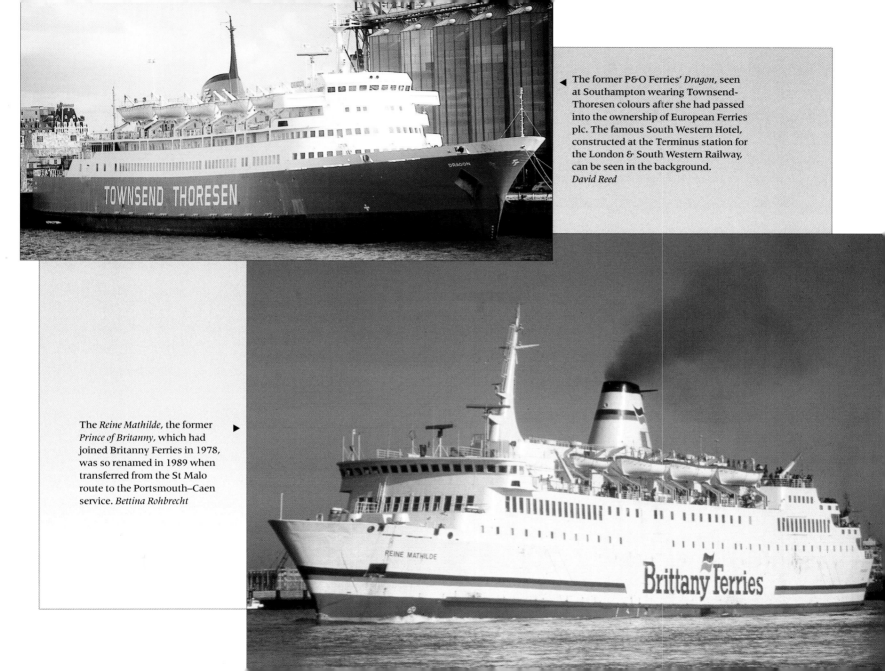

The former P&O Ferries' *Dragon*, seen at Southampton wearing Townsend-Thoresen colours after she had passed into the ownership of European Ferries plc. The famous South Western Hotel, constructed at the Terminus station for the London & South Western Railway, can be seen in the background. *David Reed*

The *Reine Mathilde*, the former *Prince of Britanny*, which had joined Britanny Ferries in 1978, was so renamed in 1989 when transferred from the St Malo route to the Portsmouth–Caen service. *Bettina Rohbrecht*

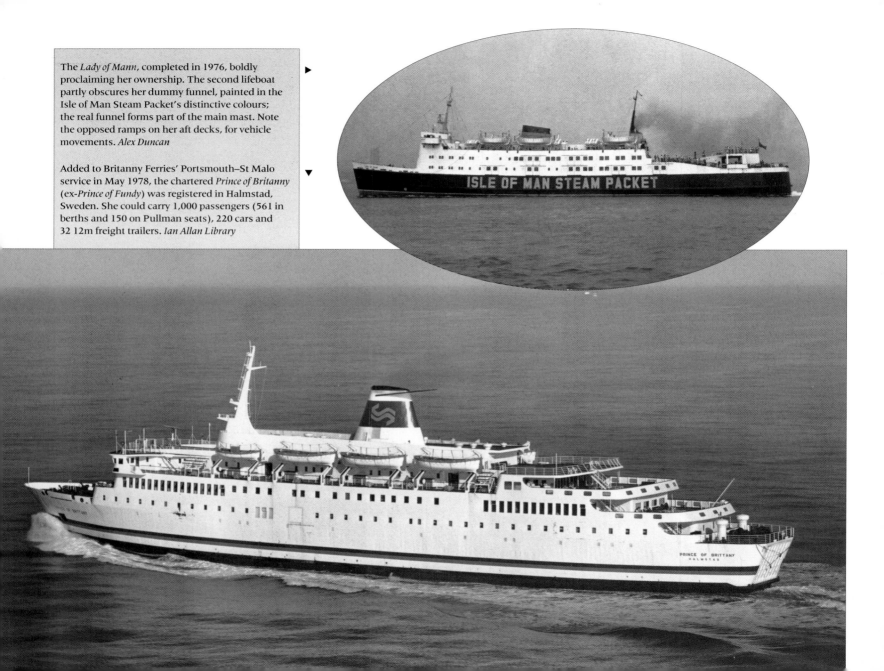

The *Lady of Mann*, completed in 1976, boldly proclaiming her ownership. The second lifeboat partly obscures her dummy funnel, painted in the Isle of Man Steam Packet's distinctive colours; the real funnel forms part of the main mast. Note the opposed ramps on her aft decks, for vehicle movements. *Alex Duncan*

Added to Britanny Ferries' Portsmouth–St Malo service in May 1978, the chartered *Prince of Britanny* (ex-*Prince of Fundy*) was registered in Halmstad, Sweden. She could carry 1,000 passengers (561 in berths and 150 on Pullman seats), 220 cars and 32 12m freight trailers. *Ian Allan Library*

6.   A NEW GENERATION FOR AN EXPANDING TRADE

Even as the old, established passenger ferry operators, state-owned as well as some private, were bringing out their first purpose-built, Ro-Ro car ferries for routes all around the UK, the vehicle-ferry revolution was already being taken a stage further. To meet the ever-expanding demand for private-car passages as well as to provide capacity for the anticipated volumes of road-haulage vehicles, a second generation of vehicle ferries began to emerge around the mid-1970s. Once again, the competition was left behind as the more radical thinkers — the new, independent operators — forged ahead with their plans for vessels that would satisfy these combined requirements.

So what were the distinguishing characteristics of the second wave of vehicle ferries? Almost without exception, they were of the drive-through configuration, but the essential difference between these ships and the preceding generation was the provision of greater vehicle deck space — in particular for many more commercial vehicles and motor coaches — and increased headroom between decks and at the points of embarkation. In effect, the ferries were linking the spreading European motorway networks, helping commercial road transportation to go international and, by so doing, making further inroads into the traditional railway business, as freight moved from track to road. Road haulage was in the ascendancy, and what had begun as a trickle was rapidly becoming a torrent. It was the day of the juggernaut, as the truck was then commonly described.

It is difficult to pinpoint which ship, precisely, qualifies as being the first of the new breed, for advances of the kind described, no matter how dramatic, still manifest themselves, from ship to ship, as a gradual process. However, among the likely contenders, on the UK routes, were two new ships for North Sea Ferries and the Townsend-Thoresen 'Super Viking' quartet which entered service from 1975.

Reflecting their greater carrying capacity, the second generation of vehicle ferries ('car ferry' no longer being an appropriate description) were much larger generally —

typically double the size of their predecessors. Ultimately, through a period of 'jumbo-isation', they would lead to the huge, multi-role super-ferries or cruise ferries that ply the UK short-sea ferry routes today.

Clearly, these new ships represented an appropriate market response to a burgeoning demand. For their owners they also offered economies of scale, because operating costs did not increase in direct proportion to size of ship. But it was not entirely a rosy picture, for concerns were being voiced increasingly, from a safety standpoint, about the direction in which ferry design was heading. The end-to-end vehicle decks of these vessels, central to the commercial effectiveness of their design, was also, potentially, their Achilles heel.

Ferries of all types and sizes are exposed throughout their lives to the same basic risks — fire, extreme weather and collision — all of which have always existed at sea, although the risk of collision is perhaps intensified because ferries generally operate in congested sea areas. However, for vehicle ferries, with open, un-partitioned garage decks, the consequences of any disaster are exacerbated by susceptibility to rapid flooding, inherently undermining all other safety and evacuation measures. The bigger the ship, moreover, the greater the scale of any calamity that may occur.

The absence of watertight sub-divisions on the exposed vehicle decks of modern ferries, especially where they are located at or below the water line, is an issue that warrants some discussion. Ranking among the worst maritime disasters ever to occur, and certainly the most documented, is the sinking of the *Titanic* in April 1912 with the loss of 1,503 lives, the result of her underwater hull being sliced open for 300ft by an iceberg. The *Titanic* was designed as a three-compartment ship: any three adjacent compartments of her hull could be flooded simultaneously without causing her to sink. In the event, the gash in her side breached five compartments. Nevertheless, she remained afloat — down at the head but on an even keel — for two and a half hours, though still, tragically, not long enough for the nearest rescuer

to reach her. By comparison, if a modern vehicle ferry, carrying as many passengers, were to sustain damage comparable to that which afflicted the *Titanic*, it could sink in just minutes and, because of lost stability, it would almost certainly heel over and capsize — a terrifying prospect.

Marine experts were anxious too that, besides the flooding hazard, other features incorporated into the design of the large vehicle ferries entering service from the mid-1970s threatened to magnify the dangers, worsening an emergency situation and turning a mishap into a tragedy. They were worried about their box-like enclosed accommodation structure, with lifeboats placed high above the water on the top deck. Equally, they were unhappy about the waterline fenders, routinely fitted to ships of this type to help rapid docking, which could interfere with lowered lifeboats or impede rescue ships coming alongside. They would have liked also to see more escape chutes installed on ships of this type.

It would take the loss of the *Herald of Free Enterprise* off Zeebrugge on 6 March 1987 to bring these messages forcibly home to an industry that, frankly, had become complacent about ferry safety. After all, there had been a sequence of earlier accidents, amounting collectively to sufficient warning to alert owners to the risks: the already described *Princess Victoria* sinking in 1953, followed by the *Heraklion* (lost off Crete on 8 December 1966), the *Wahine* (which capsized outside Wellington, New Zealand on 10 April 1968) and the *European Gateway* (which sank off Felixstowe on 19 December 1982 after colliding with the train ferry *Speedlink Vanguard*).

Of course, 10 or more years before the *Herald of Free Enterprise* disaster, nothing threatened to interrupt the development and commissioning of the new generation of passenger vehicle ferries, as companies sought to secure and then dominate their slice of the lucrative UK ferry trade. It was a period of great volatility, with numerous new ferry concerns emerging,

Salvaging the stricken *Herald of Free Enterprise* proved to be a hazardous, expensive and time-consuming operation, motivated by the urgent need to recover bodies trapped inside her. The ship had rolled over onto her beam-ends outside Zeebrugge Harbour, coming to rest on a small sandbank which prevented her from capsizing completely. But for that, the death toll in the March 1987 disaster would have been much higher.
Leo van Ginderen

a glut of construction in the shipyards and the frequent renaming of ships as they moved between owners, making it difficult to keep track of their identities.

Some of the major players of today rose to prominence during this time. DFDS, for example, which had for long maintained a steady presence in the North Sea sector (indeed, as a passenger-shipping concern of international standing) over many years, began to expand rapidly both on its UK and on its Baltic routes. The German-flag Prins Line was taken over in October 1981, becoming DFDS Prins Ferries, and just two months later DFDS absorbed the Swedish-owned Tor Line. This had first appeared on the UK ferry scene, along with other Scandinavian operators, back in the 1960s when it placed the 7,500-gross-ton, 453ft (138.1m)-long sisters *Tor Anglia* and *Tor Hollandia* in a service linking Immingham, Lincolnshire, with Gothenburg and Amsterdam from March 1967. The much larger *Tor Britannia* and *Tor Scandinavia*, like their predecessors built at the Flender Werft yard at Lübeck, succeeded this pair in 1975 and 1976 respectively, their UK terminus transferring from Immingham to Felixstowe at around this time. At 15,600 gross tons and 598ft (182.4m) in overall length, they presented a striking appearance — long, sleek lines, more like those of modern cruise ships, dominated by a single, immense funnel. The *Tor Britannia* and *Tor Scandinavia* each had a car deck area sufficient for 420 vehicles and could carry 1,268 passengers — 756 in cabins. The passenger complement was reduced when they undertook cruises.

These substantial ferries, along with others constructed from the outset for DFDS, helped to elevate its position to that of a major UK ferry operator. Noteworthy among the company's new ships were the 11,900-gross-ton *Dana Regina*, completed in July 1974, and the 14,400-gross-ton *Dana Anglia*, which made her début in May 1978, both being employed on the Esbjerg–Harwich route. The former ship, measuring 504ft (153.7m) in length

▲ The large *Tor Britannia* and her sister, *Tor Scandinavia*, had long, sleek hull lines beneath their prominent funnels. Besides their ferry duties, they spent much of the time cruising. *Bettina Rohrbrecht*

▼ The modern DFDS passenger/car ferry *Dana Anglia*, which entered service in May 1978, has an even larger funnel. *David Reed*

The vehicle and passenger ferries *Tor Anglia* and *Tor Hollandia* could each convey a maximum of 980 passengers and 300 cars or the equivalent deck-space of commercial trailers. The *Tor Anglia* is shown at the Immingham Ferry Terminal, displaying her open bow door and the ramp mechanism which, when stowed for sea, acted as a second, inner watertight enclosure. *Michael Wood*

overall, had a capacity for 250 private cars and 100 commercial vehicles, with berths for 1,006 passengers. Her later consort, also built by Aalborg Vaerft A/S, could accommodate 1,356 passengers, the majority berthed, along with 470 private cars or the equivalent space in truck numbers. As the size of the new generation of ferries continued to increase, DFDS commissioned even larger ships.

Of more modest proportions were the follow-on classes of ship brought out by Townsend-Thoresen, or the European Ferries Group, as it had become. This concern had also blossomed, acquiring the Atlantic Transport Line from the British Railways Board in November 1971, in one of the few privatisations instigated by the Conservative Government of Ted Heath. Later, in 1985, it took over much of the former P&O South Coast tonnage when the

The *Dana Anglia* leaving Harwich for Esbjerg on 26 August 1978. *G. R. Mortimer*

original P&O Ferries (the renamed Normandy Ferries) was abandoned because of heavy financial losses.

Perpetuating the trading philosophy of its principal antecedents, from 1975 European Ferries introduced its 'Super Viking' quartet — the *Viking Valiant*, *Viking Venturer*, *Viking Viscount* and *Viking Voyager* — followed from 1980 by the three ships of the 'Spirit of Free Enterprise' class, all being of roll-though layout. The 'Super Vikings' were 6,350-gross-ton ships, 422ft (128.7m) long, all built by Aalborg Vaerft. They were placed on the cross-Channel route from Southampton (later Portsmouth), supported by

The former *Viking Viscount* in service with P&O European Ferries as the *Pride of Winchester*. Two of her sisters, the *Viking Valiant* and *Viking Venturer*, were later stretched to increase their vehicle capacity by 35%, to 370 cars or the equivalent space of trucks or trailer units; this modification would also be applied to the *Free Enterprise VI* and *Free Enterprise VII* (in 1985) and to the *Spirit of Free Enterprise* (in 1991). Along with four other vessels, these five also passed to P&O ownership. *Alex Duncan*

The *Herald of Free Enterprise*, the second of a class of three sisters described as 'Blue Riband' ferries. She entered service on 1 June 1980. *Ian Allan Library*

The *Spirit of Free Enterprise*, sister ship of the ill-fated *Herald of Free Enterprise*, seen from bow and stern in drydock. For all the functionality of their design, these ships could hardly be considered visually attractive.
(both) David Reed

◄ Exemplifying the high-sided Baltic 'box-boat' design, the *Stena Normandica* leaves Ipswich bound for Rotterdam on 22 December 1977, when chartered to North Sea Ferries, prior to the delivery of *Norsky* in January 1978.
The theoretical 30min evacuation-time for ferries of this type was rarely put to the test. The *Stena Normandica* later operated on charter to Sealink (UK) on the Fishguard–Rosslare route, for which she was renamed *St. Brendan* in May 1985. Sister vessel *Stena Nordica* was chartered to Regie voor Transports Maritiem as the *Reine Astrid* from 1983 to 1986 and to SNCF as the *Versailles* from 1988. G. R. Mortimer

vessels of the 'Free Enterprise' class. Each could carry 1,327 passengers and 275 cars — a quantity that reduced if the space was allocated to commercial vehicles. Delivered in successive years, the 7,950-gross-ton *Spirit of Free Enterprise*, *Herald of Free Enterprise* and *Pride of Free Enterprise*, fabricated at the Schichau Unterweser AG shipyard at Bremerhaven, maintained services from Harwich or Dover to Zeebrugge; they provided accommodation for 1,350 (all deck passengers) and space for 350 private cars or the equivalent in lorries.

Besides its South Coast operation, which it would dispose of in 1985, P&O retained its stake in North Sea Ferries as well as its Irish Sea operations. Traffic volumes on the Hull–Rotterdam route were thriving, leading to the addition of a larger pair of second-generation ferries in 1974. Named *Norland* and *Norstar*, these sisters were built by AG 'Weser' Seebeckwerk, Bremerhaven. They were 502ft (153.0m) long, had a tonnage in excess of 12,950 gross and accommodated 1,245 passengers (173 unberthed), besides having a healthy

capacity for cars and commercial vehicles.

Of particular note among the many new operators entering the UK ferry trade in this era was Olau Lines (named after the owner, **O**laf **Lau**ritzen), which, having briefly attempted a service from Flushing to Ramsgate, in 1973 opened a Ro-Ro passenger and freight route between Flushing and Sheerness. To its inaugural ships, the company added the striking *Olau Hollandia* and *Olau Britannia* — its first new ferries — in 1981 and 1982. Following the 'box-boat' ferry style which had emanated from the Baltic, they were large vessels of 14,980 gross tons and 503ft (153.4m) overall length. Among the best-appointed short-sea ferries of their time, they too were built at Bremerhaven by AG 'Weser' Seebeckwerk. Capable of carrying 550 private cars and 1,600 passengers, they operated a daily service in either direction.

The *Olau Britannia* suffered the ignominious misfortune, on 25 August 1984, of colliding with the cargo ship *Mont Louis*, which subsequently sank. Concern at the time was

The North Sea Ferries sisters *Norland (right)* and *Norstar (below)* show off, respectively, their owner's original colour scheme and the replacement livery adopted in May 1987. *Ian Shiffman* and *Bettina Rohbrecht*

concentrated on the pollution risks from the *Mont Louis*'s cargo of radioactive material (uranium hexafluoride); had the consequences of the collision been the other way round, threatening the lives of the *Olau Britannia*'s large passenger complement, it would have been a far more serious affair.

It is reassuring to know that since 1987 the ferry industry has acted positively upon many of the recommendations of the enquiry into the *Herald of Free Enterprise* disaster and that safety standards generally have improved considerably. The issue of sub-division of vehicle decks has yet to be resolved, as any mechanism separating the deck into watertight zones would, unavoidably, interfere with loading and unloading operations. The 1990 damage stability rules for one- and two-compartment ships have certainly made a difference, some of the older ferries having buoyancy sponsons and anti-roll tanks installed in order to comply. Nevertheless, this issue remains a focus of

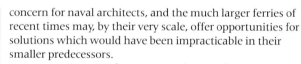

concern for naval architects, and the much larger ferries of recent times may, by their very scale, offer opportunities for solutions which would have been impracticable in their smaller predecessors.

Today we are in the era of the jumbo- or mega-ferry — the generation that since 1985 has succeeded the 'Super Vikings' and 'Spirit of Free Enterprise' classes and their contemporaries. The most recent of these vessels are far removed from the tiny ferries that resumed the short-sea crossings after 1945. As just one measure of the phenomenal increase in size that has occurred since then, P&O's latest ferries, the *Pride of Hull* and *Pride of Rotterdam*, are, at 60,600 gross tons, some 15 times the size of the *Invicta*. And marginally bigger than the White Star liner *Majestic*, which, in the 1920s, was heralded as the world's largest passenger-carrying ship!

The *Olau Britannia*, built in 1981, almost came to grief in August 1984 when she collided with the cargo ship *Mont Blanc*. As the accident occurred in deep water, it could have had far more serious consequences than the later *Herald of Free Enterprise* disaster. *David Reed*

Although, perhaps, outside the scope of this book, the *St. Patrick II* of Irish Continental Line (later Irish Ferries), with her distinctive clove-leaf funnel design, has been included here to underline the extent of ferry development on all routes connected with the British Isles. Built as the *Aurella* for Viking Line, she operated on the route from Rosslare to Cherbourg and Le Havre, being pictured at the Irish port on 11 August 1984. Also visible (on the left) is the *Innisfallen* (ex-*Connacht*) (1979) of B+I Line, with her up-and-over stern door open.
Barry Carse

7.   THE RISE AND FALL OF SEALINK

At the time of her completion the *St. George* was the largest ferry ever owned by British Railways or Sealink. Seen here backing away from the Parkeston Quay, Harwich, in July 1971, she worked the Harwich–Hook of Holland route until sold in 1984. Thereafter experiencing a varied career, she ultimately (in 2000) became the gambling ship *Texas Treasure*, based in the Gulf of Mexico. *British Railways*

Sealink was the final manifestation of state-owned shipping on the short-sea routes. It came into existence midway through the period in which the first-generation car ferries were being introduced, and fell into decline as the second-generation vessels gave way to the 'jumbo-ised' multi-role ships of the super-ferry era. On reflection it was an early example of an attempt to revamp a flagging business by reorganising its structure and adopting a new corporate image and name — a more common occurrence today. Such actions have rarely produced positive results, however — as the recent instances of Corus (British Steel) and Consignia (Royal Mail) have demonstrated — and, because it too failed to address fundamental issues, Sealink would, in the final analysis, prove no exception.

The bid to lift the UK's ailing railway shipping operations began as early as 1964, when competitive pressures were already intensifying. Indeed, it could be argued that the origins of these efforts lay in the replacement of the British Transport Commission (BTC) with the British Railways Board (BRB) — a change that occurred a year earlier, on 1 January 1963. The BRB, along with other newly-created institutions, was conceived to permit the division of responsibilities for various parts of the national transport system to make it more effective, pre-empting one of the recommendations of the *Report on the Re-Shaping of British Railways*, published just three months later, on 25 March. Commissioned by Dr Richard Beeching, Chief Executive of the BTC since June 1961, the report also proposed axing some 30% of track mileage in the British Isles, as well as phasing out steam traction. Other, equally radical measures were recommended, some of which affected railway shipping by proposing to eradicate unprofitable services.

In an effort to salvage its image and reverse its fortunes in the wake of the Beeching cuts, the railway organisation re-styled itself as 'British Rail' and adopted a modern, network-wide corporate image. This featured new-style station names and direction signs — in upper- and lower-case sans-serif lettering

— and a blue colour scheme for locomotives and ships' hulls, with a logo of opposed arrows in white on a red background (on ships carried on a red funnel) — a symbol which was to remain a familiar sight for over 20 years.

The railway ships were progressively painted in the new colours from the beginning of 1965, with the North Eastern Region's *Avalon* becoming the first new British Rail ferry delivered in this colour scheme.

Three years later, maintaining what was perceived to be a positive momentum of change, a dedicated Shipping & International Services Division was formed by BRB, one of three new divisions. As such, it was responsible for all British Rail's shipping services and ports. In keeping with the contemporary vogue, which favoured 'snappy' descriptive terms as business titles (such as 'Habitat'), the new division adopted the brand-name 'Sealink', promoting itself thereafter by this unique identity (with the exception of hovercraft services, which were operated as 'Seaspeed'). Accordingly the Sealink name was added to the corporate colour scheme introduced from 1965, being painted on all ships' sides.

The late 1960s saw the delivery of the latest British Rail car ferries, the *Antrim Princess* and *St. George*, which entered service in 1967 and 1968 respectively. The 3,630-gross-ton *Antrim Princess*, built by Hawthorn Leslie, Newcastle, was the first of a pair with striking external styling. This included an extremely long, squat funnel which, unfortunately, did not suit the Sealink logo, doing little for its general appearance. The second ship, the 3,715-gross-ton *Ailsa Princess*, built by Breda Cantieri Navali, Venice, joined her in 1971. They were placed on the Stranraer–Larne service, each conveying a maximum of 1,200 passengers and a mix of cars and heavy lorries. Their capacities were not identical, that of the *Ailsa Princess* being biased towards commercial vehicles at the expense of private cars. The *St. George* was an altogether bigger ship completed for the Harwich–Hook of Holland night service. She measured 7,356 gross tons and was 420ft long (128.0m) — some 50ft (15.2m) longer than the other pair. Her accommodation

The *Antrim Princess* at Stranraer on 6 September 1969. *John Edgington*

provided for the same number of passengers but her vehicle capacity remained low — just 220 cars and 210m of coaches or trucks. Constructed by Swan Hunter & Tyne Shipbuilders, Newcastle, the *St. George* had an overall layout and look that was to be retained for the next series of Sealink ferries. Both the *Antrim Princess* and *St. George* were completed as stern-loading ships, requiring later modification (by the addition of a bow door and ramp) to expedite vehicle handling.

It was not long before the Sealink brand-name became the marketing symbol for international railway shipping as long-standing Continental associates were encouraged to join the consortium, Zeeland Shipping Co and SNCF, along with their Belgian counterparts, all assuming the Sealink identity as constituent companies.

Zeeland had introduced its latest car ferry, the *Koningin Juliana* — an attractive, 6,682-gross-ton vessel with a length of 430ft (131.2m) — to the Hook–Harwich day service in 1968. Meanwhile, Belgian Marine was in the process of increasing its fleet of car ferries for the Ostend–Dover route with developed ships of the *Roi Baudouin* type. The company had also suffered adverse financial fortunes, exacerbated by its failure to construct ships which could better cope with the growing traffic volumes; it joined the Sealink consortium in 1970, altering its name in the following year to Regie voor Transport Maritiem (RTM) and simultaneously repainting its ships in a less attractive colour scheme which featured the company's initials in a stylised but unattractive form on their funnels.

Each of the Sealink companies brought out additional tonnage during the 1970s, their new designs gradually (albeit painfully slowly) incorporating vehicle-handling qualities that ranked with those already well-established on the ships of their privately-owned competitors. The next trio of British-flag ferries were the French-built *Hengist*, *Horsa* and *Senlac* — 5,590-gross-ton ships, 385ft (117.5m) long, with a capacity for 1,400 passengers, 217 cars and 366m of commercial vehicles. The first two, completed in 1972, entered the Folkestone– Boulogne/Ostend service; the *Senlac*, which made her maiden sailing the following season, operated between Newhaven and Dieppe in partnership with SNCF's *Valençay* and *Villandry*.

There followed two improved vessels of the *St. George* type — the *St. Edmund*, completed by Cammell Laird in 1974 for the Harwich–Hook of Holland service, and the *St. Columba*, built by Aalborg Vaerft and placed on the Holyhead–Dun Laoghaire route in 1977. Larger even than previous British Rail ships, the *St. Edmund* had a tonnage of 8,987 gross and an overall length of 428ft (130.5m), while the slightly smaller *St. Columba*, at 7,836 gross tons, measured 432ft (131.6m) in length. Both could accommodate a greater number of vehicles.

Concurrent with the British new-buildings, SNCF took delivery of the 4,556-gross-ton, 379ft (115.4m)-long *Chartres*, which was added to the Strait of Dover services from 1974, while RTM persisted with its programme of upgraded car ferries — the *Prins Philippe* in 1973 and the *Prins Laurent* the

following year. Although, at around 5,000 gross tons and 388ft (118.4m) in length, they were larger and marginally longer than the ships of the company's preceding class, their vehicle capacities remained disappointingly low, despite the fact they were fitted with a mezzanine deck. It was not until the larger *Prinses Maria Esmeralda* and *Prinses Marie Christine*, completed successively in 1974 and 1975, and the *Prins Albert*, which emerged in 1978 as the last and (at 6,019 gross tons) the largest of the series, were in service that RTM had vessels with a vehicle capacity nearer to what it truly required. All three were able to accommodate some 75% more private cars and 20% more road haulage vehicles than the previous pair.

Zeeland Steamship Co's crowning achievement in the Sealink era was the magnificent *Prinses Beatrix* of 1978, the largest vessel, at 9,238 gross tons, to operate under the Sealink banner up to that time. With a length of 430ft (131.0m) she was comparable in hull dimensions to the 10-year-old *Koningin Juliana*, but her greater size provided for 320 cars and 582m of truck space, in contrast with the earlier ship's figures of 220 cars and 210m of truck space.

From 1 January 1979 the British Railways Board reconstituted its Shipping & International Services Division as Sealink UK Ltd, a wholly-owned subsidiary. The only discernible difference occasioned by this change was that the fleet's hull colour reverted from blue to black.

Derived from the *St. Columba*, the ultimate Sealink ships of British Rail were quite superb. Though not especially elegant, their design made them ideal vehicle transporters, and they

The *Ailsa Princess* of Sealink (UK) Ltd at Weymouth, September 1982.
She transferred to the Channel Islands route earlier that season, displacing the turbine steamer *Maid of Kent*.
John Edgington

The racy *Koningin Juliana*, completed in 1968. Twenty-three years later, bound for Sardinia as the *Moby Prince* on 11 April 1991, she would sink off Livorno in southern Italy after colliding with a tanker in thick fog and being engulfed by flames when the tanker's cargo caught fire. Some 139 of her complement lost their lives in the disaster. *Ian Allan Library*

The Sealink (UK) ferry *St. Edmund* passes the Nab lightship, east of the Isle of Wight, after being requisitioned for service with the South Atlantic Task Force during the Falkland Islands conflict in May 1982. She has had a temporary helicopter pad installed aft of her funnel. *Ian Allan Library*

The *Horsa* approaches Ostend on 19 August 1980. Her sister ship, the *Hengist*, was driven ashore at Folkestone by hurricane-force winds during the great storm on 16 October 1987 but was later refloated without suffering serious damage.
Richard Capper

The Newhaven–Dieppe ferry *Senlac*, photographed in May 1974. Note the cross emblem on her funnel. After the sale of Sealink (UK) to Sea Containers 10 years later, the *Senlac* became a wholly-owned SNCF ship, ending for all time British involvement in the Newhaven–Dieppe service.
Ian Allan Library

Similar in appearance to the *Hengist*, *Horsa* and *Senlac*, the multi-role ferry *Vortigern* at Dover. This 4,371-gross-ton vessel, built at Wallsend-on-Tyne by Swan Hunter and delivered in July 1969, had capacity for 240 cars and 366 linear metres of road-haulage vehicles when not carrying rail wagons. She could also accommodate 1,000 passengers. *British Railways*

The Dubigeon-Normandie-built SNCF ferry *Chartres* at Folkestone in July 1976. She entered service in January 1974, working alongside the British Rail Sealink vessels *Horsa* and *Hengist*. The *Chartres* measured 4,800 tons gross and 379ft (115.5m) in overall length.
John Edgington

The RTM ferry *Prins Laurent*, delivered in 1974. The inwards-inclined plating of the forward bulwarks appears to have been peculiar to her and the *Prins Philippe*.
Ian Allan Library

◀ The *Prins Philippe* of 1973. Her bow door appears to have been repainted, whereas the rest of her hull has been left rust-streaked and dirty. *Bettina Rohbrecht*

were excellent passenger ships too. All were built at Belfast by Harland & Wolff, the first out, as lead-ship of the new class, being the *Galloway Princess*, which entered service on the Stranraer–Larne route in April 1980. The next three ships of the class, completed between 1980 and 1981, were the *St. Anselm*, the *St. Christopher* and the *St. David*, the first two for the Dover–Calais route and the last-named for the service from Holyhead to Dun Laoghaire. At over 7,000 gross tons, the latter trio were larger than the *Galloway Princess*, which measured 6,630 gross tons; all four had an overall length of 424ft (129.4m). Their design was characterised by split engine-room exhausts, with twin funnels placed on either side of the upper deck, providing spacious, uncluttered deck areas, benefiting both vehicle handling and the layout of the public rooms. Significantly, it was their capacity that revealed the true strength of these Sealink vessels, for, in addition to 1,000 passengers, they could accommodate 309 private cars and a substantial 780 linear metres of commercial vehicles — figures more-or-less matched by SNCF's *Côte d'Azur*, delivered in 1981 and a larger ship at 8,862 gross tons and 426ft (130.0m) in length.

But in essence, it was all too little, too late. Railway shipping, in Britain and abroad, was nearing the end of the line. For British Rail Sealink and the UK railway network as a whole,

◀ Alongside the new passenger terminal at Holyhead — then nearing completion — on 2 May 1977, the Danish-built Sealink ferry *St. Columba*. *British Railways*

which was still suffering considerable losses, the early 1980s was not a politically sympathetic time in which to impose such a blight on the beleaguered taxpayer. The new Conservative Government was committed to dismantling the framework of state subsidisation of industry, and 'privatisation' was the vogue, aimed at cutting the Exchequer's costs and paving the way for extensive tax cuts; social need was not, then, viewed as an important part of the equation. The Government shied away (then, at least) from selling-off the entire railway network into private ownership, but the railway ferry operations, not regarded as such a 'sacred cow', were a quite different proposition.

That the privatisation of railway shipping was destined to happen was confirmed by the announcement, early in 1984, that a suitable buyer had been found, in the form of Sea Containers Inc, an American firm. The deal was finalised on 18 June that year, the selling price amounting to nothing short of a gift in commercial terms. For the meagre sum of £66 million, Sea Containers had acquired 37 ships and 24 established routes plus 10 ports, complete with their harbour infrastructures, from which the services were operated.

On 27 July 1984 Sea Containers renamed the company Sealink British Ferries. A revised livery, adopted the previous March and comprising dark-blue funnel, with stylised

As a means of increasing rapidly its car-carrying capacity, British Rail Sealink acquired the *Svea Drott* of Stockholms Rederiaktieb 'Svea' in 1975 and the former *Viking II* from Townsend-Thoresen in 1977. They were renamed *Earl Godwin* and *Earl William* respectively. The *Earl Godwin* is seen off Weymouth Quay on 9 June 1979. *G. B. Wise* ▲

The *Prinses Beatrix*, another elegant Zeeland Steamship Co vessel. Built by Verolme at Heusden, she was the largest short-sea ferry on any of the UK routes when she entered service in 1978. *Ian Allan Library* ▶

Launch of the *Galloway Princess* at the Harland & Wolff shipyard, Belfast, on 24 May 1979, and *(below)* the same ship during trials in March 1980. After acceptance by Sealink (UK) she entered the Stranraer–Larne service. *(both) Ian Allan Library*

The *Earl Granville*, owned
by Sealink British Ferries,
departing Portsmouth for
Cherbourg, Guernsey and
Jersey at Easter 1986 on the
'Starliner' service. Built as
the *Viking 4* for Rederi A/B
Sally, along with two sisters,
she was acquired by Sealink
in 1981. Apart from the
words 'British Ferries' on her
side, she is unchanged from
her British Rail Sealink days.
David L. Williams

The *St. Anselm* and
St. Christopher pass one
another on their respective
crossings from Calais and
Dover. *Ian Allan Library*

The SNCF ferry *Champs
Elysées*, the last new Sealink
ferry to enter service prior to
the demise of railway
shipping under the Red
Ensign. *David Reed*

officer's ranking stripes in gold, and white hull with 'Sealink'
on the sides in blue letters, was further amended by the
simple addition of the two words 'British Ferries'.

The last Sealink ship to enter service prior to the sell-off
of British Rail's part of the consortium was the SNCF ship
Champs Elysées, delivered in October 1984 by Dubigeon-
Normandie SA, Nantes, and the first Sealink ferry to exceed
10,000 gross tons; indeed, measuring 15,093 gross tons and
427ft (130.2m) in length, she was one of the largest UK
ferries then operating, heralding the much larger ferries
that were then imminent. Barely two years later, and only
months after the demise of Sealink UK, another Sealink
partner, Zeeland, introduced the *Koningin Beatrix*, which was
double the size of the *Champs Elysees*, at 31,189 gross tons
and 531ft (161.8m) long; equipped with multiple bow and
stern doors and ramps, she was built by Van der Giessen
de Noord BV, Krimpen a/d Ijssel.

The termination of British Rail's shipping operations, which
(due to their very scale) represented the most serious aspect of
the down-turn in Sealink's fortunes, did not in itself signify
the immediate end for the other partner ferry concerns, which

continued, in various forms, for some years afterwards.
Sealink British Ferries, meanwhile, having inherited the
difficulties that beset its former, nationalised owners, would
not remain a Sea Containers company for long. On 31 May
1990 — outside the period covered by this book — it was sold
again, to Stena A/B of Sweden, becoming Sealink Stena Line,
the Sealink name finally disappearing altogether in 1995.

By 1984, when British Rail's participation in the Sealink
consortium came to an end, the traditional cross-channel
passenger ferries were little more than fading memories, and
even some of the first generation of car ferries had already
disappeared from the UK ferry routes. But it was not so much
the passing of the ships as the demise of railway shipping
under the Red Ensign that really signified the end of an era.
Once described as part of the 'complete service', it went back
over 140 years to the 1840s, when the Glasgow, Paisley &
Greenock Railway had established a ferry service on the River
Clyde and the South Eastern Railway had opened the first
railway-owned cross-Channel operation from Folkestone to
Boulogne. At its peak, in 1913, the combined British-flag
railways ferry fleet consisted of 216 vessels working routes

With the distinctive cliffs of the Kent coastline behind her, the Sealink (UK) ferry *St. Christopher* heads for Calais. *Ian Allan Library*

The 17,043-gross-ton *St. Nicholas* (ex-*Prinsessan Birgita*) sports the new Sealink corporate livery adopted in March 1984, the first ship to receive the new rig. Within four months she was the property of the privatised Sealink British Ferries concern, the name on her side being amended accordingly. Built by Gotaverken A/B, Gothenburg, she worked the Harwich–Hook run, having replaced the *St. George* and the chartered DFDS ferry *Prinz Oberon*. *Ian Allan Library*